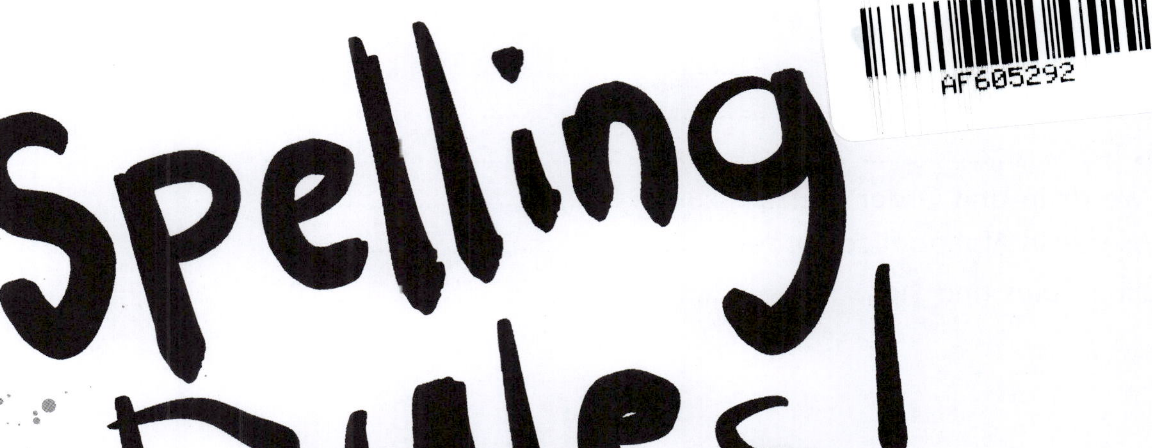

Janelle Ho and
Helen Pearson

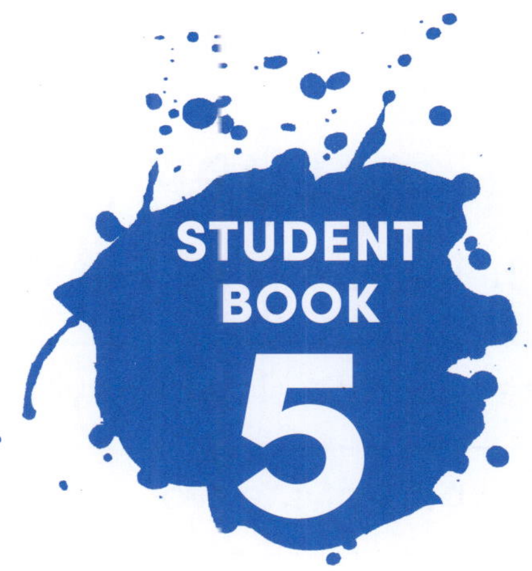

Australian Curriculum Edition

Name: ______________________________

Class: ______________________________

CONTENTS

Scope and Sequence 3
Note to Teachers and Parents 4
Units 1–35 6–75
List Words in Unit Order 76
List Words in Alphabetical Order 78
Spelling Rules and Tips 80

SLLURP

SLLURP summarises the spelling strategies that you can use to learn new words.

Say	Say the word carefully and slowly to yourself.
Listen	Listen to how each part of the word sounds in sequence.
Look	Look at the patterns of letters in the word and the shape of the word.
Understand	Understand rules, word meanings and word origins.
Remember	Remember all the similar words you can already spell and relate this knowledge to any new word.
Practise	Practise writing the word until it is firmly fixed in your long-term memory.

Scope and Sequence

UNIT	SKILL FOCUS: Letter patterns	Morphology	Etymology	Homophones/ Confusing words	Topic words	WORD LIST
1		plural suffixes: -s, -es				viruses, geniuses, biases, stitches, mattresses, quizzes, sandwiches, scarves, valleys, chimneys, factories, priorities, handkerchiefs, volcanoes, fiascos
2		irregular plurals	non-English root words	homograph: analyses		cacti, fungi, stimuli, syllabi, analyses, theses, parentheses, crises, lice, oxen, antennae, larvae, bacteria, series, species
3		-ful, -less				scornful, skilful, wilful, resentful, deceitful, delightful, suspenseful, successful, plentiful, priceless, faultless, flawless, regardless, ruthless, reckless
4	words ending in ment	-ment, -dom, -ship, -ion				instrument, experiment, implement, achievement, equipment, advertisement, boredom, wisdom, hardship, sportsmanship, censorship, insertion, hesitation, collision, aggression
5	words ending in ous	-ous	Latin and French root words			curious, conscious, anonymous, victorious, luxurious, contagious, marvellous, venomous, ridiculous, mischievous, hideous, courteous, courageous, outrageous, miscellaneous
6	REVISION					
7	ch	-logy	Greek root words			echo, scheme, chemist, monarch, scholar, chaos, chronic, chlorine, headache, architect, mechanic, technology, orchestra, archaeology, arachnophobia
8		-al, -ic, -ally			adverbs of frequency	mineral, medical, occasional, official, hysterical, historical, artificial, identical, exceptional, eventual, tragic, automatic, sympathetic, aquatic, rhythmic
9		-able, -ible	word families	illegible/eligible		reliable, capable, adorable, available, comfortable, miserable, valuable, horrible, terrible, sensible, flexible, impossible, invisible, eligible, illegible
10	double consonants			current/currant, assess/excess	occupations	opposite, different, applause, intelligent, excess, apparent, accidental, immediate, occupation, exaggerate, community, parallel, cannibal, innovative, affectionate
11					acronyms, blends, eponyms	scuba, radar, sonar, laser, smog, heliport, lamington, diesel, bikini, braille, pasteurised, silhouette, guillotine, saxophone, valentine
12	REVISION					
13	aw, or, au, augh			aural/oral		gawky, awkward, ordinary, organise, orphan, original, orchard, ornament, orthodontist, naughty, aural, audible, audition, exhaustion, authentic
14		com-, con-, anti-				combine, companion, commemorate, comprehend, compel, conceal, concentrate, condescending, conference, consequence, antiseptic, antibiotic, anticlimax, antisocial, anticlockwise
15		im-, in-, ir-, il-		illegal/illegible/ eligible		imperfect, impatient, impractical, immature, insane, inappropriate, inconvenient, incapable, indigestible, irregular, irrelevant, irresponsible, irresistible, illegal, illogical
16		multiple affixes	word families			excellence, undeserved, reassuring, irresponsibly, unembarrassed, knowledgeably, acknowledgement, imaginative, dependable, discontentment, misfortunes, inconveniently, disastrously, fascination, misbehaviour
17			non-English words		colours	kiwi, batik, trek, yoga, bazaar, mandarin, spaghetti, kayak, moccasin, tsunami, sushi, kimono, bonsai, karate, origami, bouquet, camouflage, corroboree, llama, poncho
18	REVISION					
19	qu					aqua, liquid, frequent, quality, quantity, quiver, conquest, acquire, adequate, tranquil, eloquent, quotation, quarantine, inquisitive, acquaintance
20	words ending in gue, que			plague/plaque		tongue, rogue, plague, colleague, fatigue, intrigue, dialogue, catalogue, synagogue, unique, antique, technique, boutique, mosque, plaque
21	ui			sweet/suite, suit/ suite, crews/cruise		fluid, ruin, suitcase, guide, guilty, biscuit, pursuit, suitable, guitar, inquire, bruise, intuition, nuisance, mosquito, circuit
22	our				Australian and American spelling differences	flour, course, flavour, favourite, colourful, humour, harbour, journal, nourish, honour, odour, mournful, detour, behaviour, tournament
23			Latin and Greek root words			popular, manual, library, inhabit, universe, delicate, circular, equator, benefit, democracy, dependent, monotonous, microscope, magnificent, contradict
24	REVISION					
25		different prefixes	*mittere, premere, ferre*			admit, permit, submit, emit, impress, compress, repress, suppress, offer, refer, prefer, infer, confer, suffer, transfer
26	y as a vowel sound					type, byte, rhyme, myth, gypsy, rhythm, oxygen, symbol, synthetic, typical, pyjamas, physician, sympathy, century, tragedy
27		-ty, -ity				variety, poverty, charity, creativity, simplicity, sincerity, personality, maturity, majority, minority, electricity, familiarity, speciality, opportunity, authority
28	words ending in ant, ent	-ant, -ent		dependant/ dependent		brilliant, ignorant, dominant, tolerant, hesitant, dependant, redundant, obedient, consistent, incident, permanent, sufficient, efficient, coherent, imminent
29	words ending in ance, ence	-ance, -ence		conscience/ conscious		distance, balance, assistance, resistance, significance, reluctance, insurance, surveillance, maintenance, influence, experience, violence, existence, evidence, conscience
30	REVISION					
31	sh sound: s, ch, sch, si, ci, ti, ss, sci, xi words ending in tious, cious	-tial, -cial				machinery, schedule, tissue, tension, ferocious, suspicious, appreciate, luscious, commercial, initiate, confidential, influential, complexion, ambitious, conscientious
32			German words			noodle, hamburger, schnitzel, strudel, muesli, pretzel, delicatessen, kindergarten, abseil, blitz, rucksack, wanderlust, uber, kaput, waltz
33	silent letters					gnome, gnaw, pneumonia, pterodactyl, psychology, subtle, succumb, solemn, receipt, resign, island, handsome, exhibit, knack, playwright
34		mono-, multi-, omni-, poly-			number prefixes	monopoly, monolith, monologue, monosyllabic, multiple, multipurpose, multimedia, multicultural, multilingual, polygon, polyphonic, omnivore, omnipresent, omnipotent, omniscient
35	REVISION					

NOTE TO TEACHERS AND PARENTS

Spelling Rules!

Some students are natural spellers. But the vast majority of students need formal, systematic and sequential instruction about the way spelling works and the strategies they can use to become independent, confident spellers and spelling risk-takers.

The *Spelling Rules!* program is based on sound linguistic and pedagogical theory. It is informed by research into how students of different ages acquire and apply spelling skills, and how those skills move from the working to the long-term memory. The program closely follows the Australian English curriculum. *Australian Curriculum: English* references are provided in the Teacher Resource Books. The program consists of seven student books, fully supported by two Teacher Resource Books.

Each student book contains units of work, with each unit designed to be used over the course of a week. The content of each unit simultaneously develops new skills and reinforces skills from previous units and earlier books. The introduction of new letter patterns is logically sequenced and takes into account both frequency of use and complexity. Where appropriate, topic words from other curriculum areas such as mathematics, science and social sciences are included. When spelling rules are introduced, only known sounds and letter patterns are used so that students focus on one skill at a time. Regular revision units enable teachers to assess student progress and reinforce key rules and patterns from previous units.

Spelling knowledge

Learning to spell involves developing different kinds of spelling knowledge. In many cases, particularly in the upper grades, more than one kind of knowledge is called upon at a time. As they work through the activities in each *Spelling Rules!* unit, students will develop:

- **Kinaesthetic knowledge** – the physical feeling when saying different sounds and words, and when writing the shapes of letters and words
- **Phonological knowledge** – how a word sounds and the patterns of sounds in words
- **Visual knowledge** – how letters and words look and the visual patterns in words
- **Morphemic knowledge** – the meaning or function of words or parts of words
- **Etymological knowledge** – the origins and history of words and the effect this has on spelling patterns.

Icons used in Student Book 5

This icon highlights useful spelling rules. The rule is always introduced the first time students will need it to complete an activity. There is also a handy summary of important rules on page 80.

This icon tells students that a special clue or hint is provided for an activity. It may be a spelling, grammar or punctuation convention, or a definition of a useful term.

Student Book 5

Units of work

Student Book 5 contains 35 weekly units of work. See the **Scope and Sequence chart** on page 3 for more information. Each revision unit gives students an opportunity to self-assess.

Word lists

In *Student Book 5*, each unit (except Revision) has a list of spelling words. The core words in the lists have been chosen to support the learning focus and strategies being taught in the unit.

Spelling lists enable a spelling element to be focused on, and provide sufficient examples to consolidate the teaching point. Topic words come from other curriculum areas, such as mathematics and social sciences. In addition, homophones and words that are easily confused with each other are explained and practised.

SLLURP

Each word list begins with a reminder for students to SLLURP. SLLURP summarises the strategies that will help spelling move from students' working memory to their long-term memory. These strategies are provided on page 2, for easy reference.

Unit at a glance

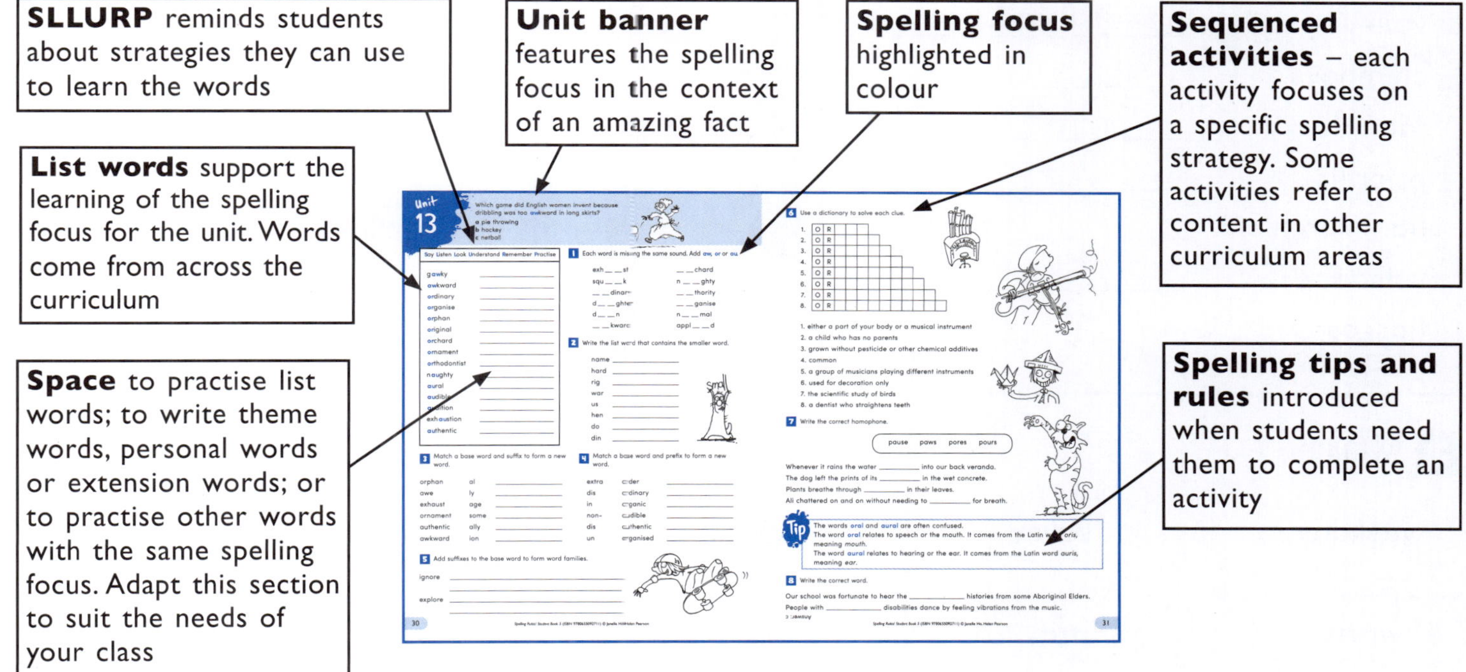

Spelling Rules! Teacher Resource Book 3–6

Full teacher support for *Student Book 5* is provided by *Spelling Rules! Teacher Resource Book 3–6*. Here you will find valuable background information about spelling development and spelling knowledge, along with practical resources, such as:

- teaching tips for every unit in *Student Book 5*
- extra word lists
- strategies for teaching spelling
- guidelines for assessment and diagnosis of errors
- activities to support struggling spellers
- worthwhile extension for more able spellers.

Unit 1

Which of these activities is performed in circuses?

a lawn bowls
b tight-rope walking
c loose-rope waddling

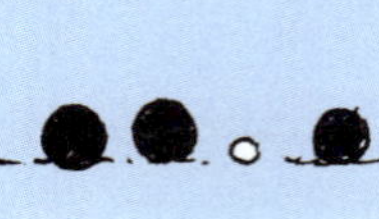

Say Listen Look Understand Remember Practise

viruses	______
geniuses	______
biases	______
stitches	______
mattresses	______
quizzes	______
sandwiches	______
scarves	______
valleys	______
chimneys	______
factories	______
priorities	______
handkerchiefs	______
volcanoes	______
fiascos	______

Rule

If a noun ends in **s**, **ss**, **ch**, **sh**, **x** or **z**, add **es** to form the plural.
Exceptions:
- *quizzes* (double the **z** before adding **es**)
- If **ch** makes a hard **c** sound, just add **s**.

1 Write the plural ending for each noun.

bus___	witness___	quiz___
ostrich___	waltz___	fox___
stomach___	rash___	monarch___
mattress___	stitch___	circus___

Rule

If a noun ends in a vowel + **y**, add **s** to form the plural.
highway → *highways*
If a noun ends in a consonant + **y**, change the **y** to **i** and add **es** to form the plural.
copy → *copies*   *berry* → *berries*

2 Write the plural.

weekday	valley	mystery	chimney	factory
______	______	______	______	______
worry	tray	buoy	priority	trophy
______	______	______	______	______

3 Write the singular.

kidneys	abilities	decoys	allergies	mazes
______	______	______	______	______
biases	crutches	viruses	headaches	
______	______	______	______	

Spelling Rules! Student Book 5 (ISBN 9780655092711) © Janelle Ho, Helen Pearson

Nouns that end in **o** usually add **es** to form the plural. *mosquitoes*
Some exceptions: foreign words (*kimonos*), abbreviations (*rhinos*) and words ending in two vowels (*videos*).

4 Circle the correct plural form.

radios
radioes

potatos
potatoes

flamingos
flamingoes

banjos
banjoes

photos
photoes

mosquitos
mosquitoes

Rule

Nouns that end in **f** usually change the **f** to **v** before adding **es** to form the plural.
half → *halves*
All nouns ending in **ff**, and some nouns ending in **f**, just add **s** to form the plural.
cliffs *gulfs* *chiefs*

5 Rewrite these sentences, making the nouns plural. Change other words when necessary.

One puff of wind blew the scarf away.

____

The wolf knocked the knife off the shelf.

____

At the wharf, a woman waves her handkerchief in a farewell gesture.

____

Eponyms are words that were originally the name of a person or place.
Braille is a writing system named after its inventor, Louis Braille.

7 Match each words to its origin.

sandwich rugby marathon pavlova diesel boycott cardigan

snack named after an earl who was too busy to eat a proper meal _______________

meringue-based dessert named after a Russian ballerina _______________

long race named after a place in ancient Greece _______________

game where you run with a ball, named after a school in England _______________

a knitted sweater or jacket named after an earl _______________

a type of fuel used for engines, named after a German engineer _______________

the action of refusing to buy or use something, named after an Irish landowner _______________

Answer: b

Unit 2

Which of these animals have **antennae**?

a bees
b bulls
c deer

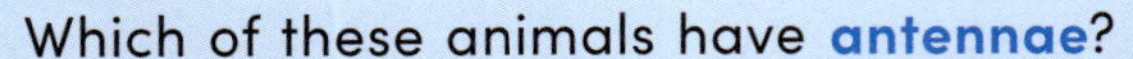

Say Listen Look Understand Remember Practise	
cacti	______
fungi	______
stimuli	______
syllabi	______
analyses	______
theses	______
parentheses	______
crises	______
lice	______
oxen	______
antennae	______
larvae	______
bacteria	______
series	______
species	______

Tip Some words change the vowel or vowels to show the plural.

Tip Some nouns of Greek origin that end in **us** change **us** to **i**. *cactus* → *cacti*
Exceptions:
octopus → *octopi* or *octopuses*
hippopotamus → *hippopotami* or *hippopotamuses*

1 Write the plural.

fungus ______ syllabus ______

stimulus ______ focus ______

octopus ______ hippopotamus ______

2 Write the plural.

thesis ______ hypothesis ______

Tip Some nouns of Greek origin that end in **is** change **is** to **es**. *crisis* → *crises*

3 Write the singular.

parentheses ______ analyses ______

Tip Some nouns of Latin origin that end in **a** add **e**.
larva → *larvae*

4 Write the plural.

larva ______ antenna ______ vertebra ______

5 Write the plural. Explain the tip you used.

oasis ______ ______

Spelling Rules! Student Book 5 (ISBN 9780655092711) © Janelle Ho, Helen Pearson

6 Write the plural of these words of Old English origin.

louse is from the Old English word *lus.* ________________

mouse is from the Old English word *mus.* ________________

ox is from the Old English word *oxa.* ________________

sheep is from the Old English word *sceap.* ________________

deer is from the Old English word *deor.* ________________

tooth is from the Old English word *tof.* ________________

foot is from the Old English word *fot.* ________________

man is from the Old English word *man.* ________________

woman is from the Old English word *wimman.* ________________

child is from the Old English word *cild.* ________________

Tip Some nouns of Latin origin that end in **um** change **um** to **a**. *curriculum* → *curricula*

7 Write the plural.

bacterium	stratum	ovum	millennium
________	________	________	________

8 Circle the words that are the same in their singular and plural forms. Underline the words that are of Latin origin.

military	species	sheep	hippopotamus	salmon
cattle	chef	shrimp	moose	crisis

9 What will help you work out what the plural word is?

____

____

____

____

____

____

____

____

____

____

____

Answer: a

Unit 3

Which of these animals can be trained to be skil**ful** surfers?

a pandas
b cows
c dogs

Say **L**isten **L**ook **U**nderstand **R**emember **P**ractise

scorn**ful** __________
skil**ful** __________
wil**ful** __________
resent**ful** __________
deceit**ful** __________
delight**ful** __________
suspense**ful** __________
success**ful** __________
plenti**ful** __________
price**less** __________
fault**less** __________
flaw**less** __________
regard**less** __________
ruth**less** __________
reck**less** __________

Tip Adding the suffix **ful** or **less** sometimes changes the spelling of the base word.
pity → pitiful, pitiless

1 Write the base word for these adjectives.

skilful ________ wilful ________

beautiful ________ plentiful ________

awful ________ penniless ________

2 Group the base words of these adjectives.

countless suspenseful deceitful
forgetful flawless resentful

base word = noun	base word = verb

3 Write a list word that rhymes.

toothless ________ backless ________
insightful ________ mournful ________

4 The base words of *ruthless* and *reckless* are no longer in use. Make a guess as to what the base words mean. Then use a dictionary to check your answers.

	your guess	dictionary definition
ruth		
reck		

5 Write a list word that is a synonym.

mocking ________ precious ________ anyway ________
stubborn ________ insincere ________ bitter ________

Antonyms are words that are opposite in meaning.
Antonyms can be made by:

- adding a prefix *helpful → unhelpful*
- changing the suffix. *careful → careless*

6 Write an antonym for each word.

successful ____________ grateful ____________ thoughtful ____________

joyful ____________ harmful ____________ useful ____________

7 Make an adverb by adding **ly** to each adjective. Use each adverb in a sentence.

skilful ____________

____

____

successful ____________

____

____

Words for quantities sometimes end in **ful**.
cupful

8 Use a word with the suffix **ful** to complete each sentence.

Uncle Jim refuses to drink tea unless it has a ____________ of sugar in it.

It should take only one ____________ of water to wash a car.

Che took one ____________ of milk and spat it out. It was sour!

9 Proofread this recount. The recount has five words that are incorrect. Circle the mistakes. Then write the correct spelling of the words in the boxes.

Mrs Jones, our neighbour, is over 80 but she is still quite energetic. Yesterday she waved cheerfuly as she hurried passed on her way to the shops. A few seconds later, I heard her call out in pain. Had she been wreckless? We found her lying on the ground with an awful lot of blood dripping down her leg. Mum took her to the doctor and the cut needed five stitchs. Mrs Jones was greatful that we were nearby when she needed help.

Answer: c

Unit 4

What is the greatest depth underwater that a diver has ever gone without any breathing equip**ment**?

a 40 metres
b 2000 metres
c 200 metres

Say **L**isten **L**ook **U**nderstand **R**emember **P**ractise

instru**ment**	______
experi**ment**	______
imple**ment**	______
achieve**ment**	______
equip**ment**	______
advertise**ment**	______
bore**dom**	______
wis**dom**	______
hard**ship**	______
sportsman**ship**	______
censor**ship**	______
insert**ion**	______
hesitat**ion**	______
collis**ion**	______
aggress**ion**	______

1 Write a list word for each clue.

it tries to sell you something ______
a difficult situation to endure ______
try things out ______
a tool ______
use this to make music ______
something added ______
hostile action ______

2 Write the list word that contains the smaller word.

strum ______
port ______
sit ______
tis ______
eve ______
rim ______
red ______

Tip The suffixes **ment**, **dom**, **ship** and **hood** all form nouns.
The base word does not usually change when **ment**, **dom**, **ship** or **hood** are added.

3 Add **ment**, **dom**, **ship** or **hood** to each word to form the noun.

free______	leader______	child______	advertise______
champion______	achieve______	hard______	equip______
king______	employ______	govern______	adult______

4 Write the base word for each noun. Circle the word if the spelling of the base word has changed.

wisdom	censorship	argument	boredom
______	______	______	______

Spelling Rules! Student Book 5 (ISBN 9780655092711) © Janelle Ho, Helen Pearson

Synonyms are words with the same or similar meanings.
grateful and *thankful* are synonyms.

5 Use a dictionary to find a synonym.

collision	disagreement	boredom	amazement
______________	______________	______________	______________

Some words ending in **ment** can function as both nouns and verbs.
Look at the <u>document</u>. (noun) *You should <u>document</u> the process.* (verb)

6 Use each word in a sentence as a noun and as a verb.

experiment	(noun) ______________________________
	(verb) ______________________________
compliment	(noun) ______________________________
	(verb) ______________________________
implement	(noun) ______________________________
	(verb) ______________________________

7 Rewrite each sentence using a list word.

Elders have knowledge and experience and are rightly looked up to.

____

Emil wasn't sure about what to do next and as a result, he failed to score a goal.

____

When two or more words start with the same sound, it is called **alliteration**.
Jack danced a jolly jig when he got the joyful news.

8 Add a descriptive word to complete these alliterations. Write your own alliterative sentence.

Charlie cheerfully challenged the ______________ champion.
Debbie was ______________ disappointed to miss the dance.
Ann accepted the award in ______________ amazement.
Erin ______________ explained her experiment to the visiting expert.

____

Answer: c

Unit 5

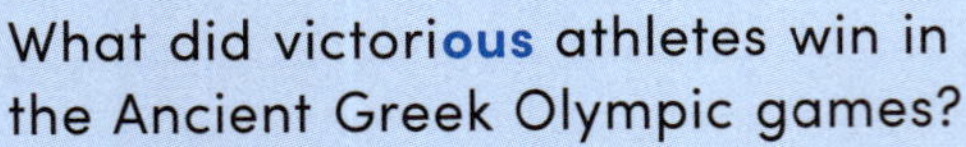

What did victor**ous** athletes win in the Ancient Greek Olympic games?

a a wreath of olive leaves
b a basket of pine cones
c a pie in the face

Say Listen Look Understand Remember Practise	
curi**ous**	________
consci**ous**	________
anonym**ous**	________
victori**ous**	________
luxuri**ous**	________
contagi**ous**	________
marvell**ous**	________
venom**ous**	________
ridicul**ous**	________
mischiev**ous**	________
hide**ous**	________
courte**ous**	________
courage**ous**	________
outrage**ous**	________
miscellane**ous**	________

Words that end in **ous** are adjectives.

1 Complete the table.

noun	adjective
	religious
caution	
	mischievous
marvel	
	hazardous
curiosity	
	anxious
venom	
	ambitious
danger	

If the base word ends in **e**, drop the **e** before adding **ous**.
fame → *famous*
Exception: words ending in **ce** or **ge**.

If the base word ends in **our**, drop the **u** before adding **ous**.
humour → *humorous*

2 Add the suffix **ous**.

adventure ________

nerve ________

ridicule ________

carnivore ________

3 Add the suffix **ous**.

glamour ________

vigour ________

rigour ________

odour ________

Tip If the base word ends in **ce** or **y**, change the **e** or **y** to **i** before adding **ous**.
space → spacious *vary → various*

4 Add the suffix **ous**.

envy ______ space ______ glory ______
vice ______ luxury ______ fury ______
grace ______ mystery ______ victory ______

Etymology is the study of word origins.
Many English words have their origins in words from other languages.

5 Write a word ending in **ous** that comes from each word.

furious outrageous curious precious delicious courageous

Delicia is the Latin word for delight. ______
Outre is the old French word meaning beyond. ______
Furia is the Latin word for rage. ______
Precios is an old French word meaning costly. ______
Cor is the Latin word for heart. ______
Curios is the old French word for anxious. ______

6 Write a synonym ending in **ous**. Choose two to use in a sentence.

angry ______ contagious ______ brave ______
envious ______ hazardous ______ successful ______

______

______

Comparative adjectives compare two things.
*My young**er** sister is **more** adventurous than I am.*
Superlative adjectives compare three or more things.
*The small**est** spiders can also be the **more** venomous.*

7 Complete the tables.

adjective	comparative form
wealthy	
beautiful	
curious	

adjective	superlative form
simple	
dangerous	
useful	

Answer: a

Lawnmower motors were once a use**ful** addition to the equipment used in which sport?

a horse racing
b triathlon
c karting

1 Add a suffix to each word. Group the new words.

success	dom
argue	ous
wise	ful
humour	ship
champion	hood
luxury	ment
mischief	
leader	

Nouns

______________ ______________
______________ ______________

Adjectives

______________ ______________
______________ ______________

2 Write the plural.

patch	stimulus	factory	crisis	box
______	______	______	______	______
quiz	**species**	**wolf**	**stomach**	**volcano**
______	______	______	______	______

3 Use the clues to make a word.

furious + c ______________ precious + v ______________

humorous + n + e ______________ courteous + a + g ______________

a ment ______________ con ious ______________

de ful ______________ neighbour ______________

pe  ful ______________ s ful ______________

g eful ______________  ker  ______________

Spelling Rules! Student Book 5 (ISBN 9780655092711) © Janelle Ho, Helen Pearson

4 Use the clues to complete the puzzle.

								F	U	L
								F	U	L
								F	U	L
								F	U	L
								F	U	L
								F	U	L
								F	U	L

1. terrible
2. wanting one's own way
3. causes injury
4. mocking
5. dishonest
6. very pleasant
7. nail-biting

5 These pairs of words are synonyms. One word in each pair has a spelling error. Circle the misspelt word and write it correctly as part of a noun group. For example: *a ridiculous costume.*

poisonous – venormous ____________________________

riddiculous – foolish ____________________________

anxous – worried ____________________________

marvellous – brillient ____________________________

humourous – amusing ____________________________

6 The word analyses is both a verb and a noun. Answer the questions.

analyses as a verb:

Circle the correct pronunciation. /an-u-lai-zus/ /uh-nal-uh-seez/

Write the base word. __________________

analyses as a noun:

Circle the correct pronunciation. /an-u-lai-zus/ /uh-nal-uh-seez/

Write the singular noun. __________________

7 Replace the phrases with an adverb ending in **ly**.

Tom ______________ (without signing his name) wrote a rhyming poem about his teacher, Ms Cross. The poem was ______________ (with humour) worded and praised Ms Cross. Tom left the poem on his teacher's desk. Later he watched ______________ (with anxiety) as Ms Cross read the poem ______________ (with care). His teacher looked at Tom and smiled ______________ (with mischief).

'Tom wrote this fine poem extremely well.
That he is a poet is easy to tell,
For in making jokes does our Tom excel.
It's such a shame he's not learnt to spell!'

Answer: c

Unit 7

Modern technology is used to measure the speed of the serve in which sport?

a figure skating
b tea parties
c tennis

Say Listen Look Understand Remember Practise

echo	________
scheme	________
chemist	________
monarch	________
scholar	________
chaos	________
chronic	________
chlorine	________
headache	________
architect	________
mechanic	________
technology	________
orchestra	________
archaeology	________
arachnophobia	________

1 Colour the circle blue if **ch** makes the sound in **ch**ip.
Colour the circle red if **ch** sounds like **k**.
Colour the circle green if **ch** sounds like **sh**.

ache	◯	reach	◯
stomach	◯	chemist	◯
machine	◯	anchor	◯
champion	◯	character	◯
scheme	◯	charades	◯
zucchini	◯	parachute	◯

2 Fill in the missing vowels to make list words.

sch __ m __	__ rch __ str __
m __ n __ rch	h __ __ d __ ch __
ch __ __ s	chr __ n __ c
ch __ m __ st	__ rch __ __ __ l __ gy
__ ch __	t __ chn __ l __ gy

3 Write a word with a hard **ch** (sounds like **k**).

a group of singers	________
a designer of buildings	________
an internal organ	________
a pupil	________
a person in a story	________
used to purify pool water	________
someone who fixes machines	________
used to moor a ship	________

4 Write the plural.

echo	________
chorus	________
ache	________
orchestra	________
technology	________
stomach	________
chemist	________
chaos	________

5 Some English words are related to Greek words. Use a dictionary to find English words beginning with a hard **ch** (sounds like **k**) that are related to these Greek words.

1.	C	H		R									
2.	C	H				E							
3.	C	H							E				
4.	C	H							S				
5.	C	H											M

1. choros = song and dance
2. chroma = colour
3. chronikos = to do with time
4. chrysallis = golden case
5. chrysanthemon = golden flower

6 Draw a line to match each **logy** word to its meaning.

meteorology	the study of the mind and behaviour
archaeology	the study of poisons
psychology	the study of animals
geology	the study of living things
biology	the study of rocks and minerals
zoology	the study of the past by digging up buried objects
cosmology	the study of word origins
toxicology	the study of the origins of the universe
etymology	the study of weather

What does **logy** mean? ______________________________

____

7 Join these simple sentences into one logical sentence using the word or words indicated.

I had an earache. I went to the chemist to buy some drops. (so)

____

Rachel is an archaeologist. Rachel spends a lot of time overseas. (who)

____

The searchers were able to accurately locate the ancient anchor. They used modern technology. (by using)

____

____

Answer: c

Unit 8

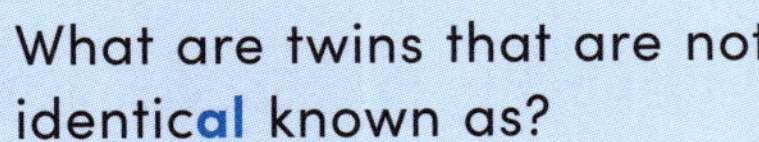

What are twins that are not identical known as?

a fraternal twins
b maternal twins
c paternal twins

Say Listen Look Understand Remember Practise

mineral	______
medical	______
occasional	______
official	______
hysterical	______
historical	______
artificial	______
identical	______
exceptional	______
eventual	______
tragic	______
automatic	______
sympathetic	______
aquatic	______
rhythmic	______

1 Make words ending in **al**. Group them according to the number of syllables you hear.

al: medic, tropic, identic, vertic, logic, music, chemic, hysteric, historic

3 syllable words

______ ______
______ ______
______ ______

4 syllable words

______ ______
______

2 Complete the tables.

noun	adjective
medicine	
	tropical
culture	
	exceptional
identity	

noun	adjective
	logical
occasion	
	tragic
aqua	
	sympathetic

3 Circle the words when **al** is a suffix and not part of the base word.

metal electrical magical hospital principal
alphabetical interval optical actual political

Spelling Rules! Student Book 5 (ISBN 9780655092711) © Janelle Ho, Helen Pearson

Most words that end in **ic** add **al** and **ly** to form the adverb.
magic → *magically*
Exception: *public* → *publicly*

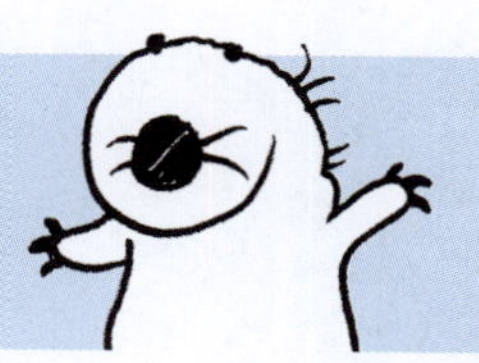

4 Change each adjective to an adverb.

tragic ____________________ historic ____________________
heroic ____________________ automatic ____________________
sarcastic ____________________ public ____________________

5 These adverbs show frequency. Write them in order from most to least frequent.

usually never rarely always occasionally often

most frequent

____
____
____
____
____
____

least frequent

6 Complete each sentence using an antonym of the word in brackets.

The flowers looked beautiful but a sign said they were ________________. (real)
The gymnasts each had an ________________ length of time to warm up. (different)
I had to rewrite my story because the ending was ________________. (logical)
Students whose achievements are ________________ are recognised at an assembly. (average)

7 These words are sometimes confused. Use each word in a sentence.

hysterical	____________________
historical	____________________
vertical	____________________
horizontal	____________________
identical	____________________
identifiable	____________________

Answer: a

Unit 9

Augie the world-record-holding dog is cap**able** of holding how many tennis balls in his mouth?

a three
b five
c twelve

Say Listen Look Understand Remember Practise

reli**able**	______
cap**able**	______
ador**able**	______
avail**able**	______
comfort**able**	______
miser**able**	______
valu**able**	______
horr**ible**	______
terr**ible**	______
sens**ible**	______
flex**ible**	______
imposs**ible**	______
invis**ible**	______
elig**ible**	______
illeg**ible**	______

1 Add **ible** or **able** to make a list word.

reli______ sens______
invis______ flex______
ador______ terr______
cap______ miser______
comfort______ valu______

2 Draw a line to match each adjective to its meaning. Use a dictionary if you need help.

edible	able to be carried
visible	able to be heard
legible	able to be understood
audible	able to be eaten
portable	able to be seen
inflatable	able to be read
intelligible	able to be filled with air

3 Complete the table to build word families.

noun	adjective	adverb
reliability		reliably
	valuable	
capability		
	comfortable	
		terribly
	invisible	
	miserable	
responsibility		

Spelling Rules! Student Book 5 (ISBN 9780655092711) © Janelle Ho, Helen Pearson

If the base word ends in silent **e**, the **e** is usually dropped before adding **ible** or **able**.
believable *collapsible*
Keep the **e** to keep the soft **c** or soft **g** sound. *noticeable* *changeable*

4 Change each verb to an adjective by adding **able**.

desire ____________
admire ____________
forgive ____________
notice ____________
consider ____________
profit ____________

5 Change each verb to an adjective by adding **ible**.

response ____________
sense ____________
collapse ____________
submerse ____________
reverse ____________
flex ____________

6 Add a suitable adjective that ends in **able** or **ible**.

a ____________ chair
an ____________ journey
a ____________ nappy
a ____________ friend
an ____________ baby
a ____________ shock
a ____________ seatbelt
a ____________ organiser

7 Complete each sentence by adding a prefix to the word in brackets to make the antonym.

The old sofa was very ____________. (comfortable)
The voice on the other end of the phone was ____________. (mistakable)
My brother even destroys toys that are guaranteed to be ____________! (destructible)
The deep snow made the road ____________. (passable)
Yusef is ____________ of seeing a ball without throwing or kicking it. (capable)

8 These words are sometimes confused. Use a dictionary to write a definition for each word.
Write a sentence using each word.

illegible definition ____________
in a sentence ____________
____

eligible definition ____________
in a sentence ____________
____

Answer: b

Unit 10

What is the longest time that someone has juggled a football with their feet, non-stop?

a three and a half years
b 45 minutes
c 7 hours, 5 minutes and 25 seconds

BOING BOING BOING BOING

Say Listen Look Understand Remember Practise

opposite ______
different ______
applause ______
intelligent ______
excess ______
apparent ______
accidental ______
immediate ______
occupation ______
exaggerate ______
community ______
parallel ______
cannibal ______
innovative ______
affectionate ______

1 Group the list words according to the number of syllables you hear.

2 syllables ______ ______ ______

3 syllables ______ ______ ______ ______

4 syllables ______ ______ ______ ______ ______ ______ ______ ______

2 Write the list word that is a synonym.

job ______ now ______
new ______ obvious ______

3 The sound **c** makes can be hard (one sound) or soft (two sounds). Colour the square if **cc** makes one sound. Colour the circle if **cc** makes two sounds.

☐ ◯ accurate	☐ ◯ accent	☐ ◯ occupy
☐ ◯ occur	☐ ◯ success	☐ ◯ eccentric
☐ ◯ accuse	☐ ◯ occasion	☐ ◯ broccoli

4 Draw lines to illustrate the meaning of each word.

parallel vertical horizontal intersecting converging

5 Complete the tables.

adjective	noun
different	
	accident
affectionate	
	intelligence

verb	noun
	applause
exaggerate	
	announcement
embarrass	

6 Complete the crossword by naming each occupation.

Across

2. works with precious metals and stones
7. learns a trade
10. drives passengers in a car
11. draws pictures for books

Down

1. sells fruit and vegetables
3. designs structures and machines
4. a member of a local council
5. keeps accounts
6. represents their country
8. a teacher and researcher at a university
9. someone who helps others

7 The words *excess* and *access* are commonly confused. Match the word to the correct definition. Then write the correct word to complete the sentence.

excess — an abnormal amount; surplus

access — the right of entry; an entrance

Shake off the ______________ flour before frying the chicken pieces.

Only teachers have ______________ to the sick bay.

Answer: c

Unit 11

What do the letters in the word '**scuba**' stand for?

a **s**elf-**c**ontained **u**nderwater **b**reathing **a**pparatus
b **s**illy **c**ats **u**nderstand **b**army **a**pes
c **s**ea **c**raft **u**pper **b**reathing **a**ir

Say **L**isten **L**ook **U**nderstand **R**emember **P**ractise

scuba	__________
radar	__________
sonar	__________
laser	__________
smog	__________
heliport	__________
lamington	__________
diesel	__________
bikini	__________
braille	__________
pasteurised	__________
silhouette	__________
guillotine	__________
saxophone	__________
valentine	__________

1 Write a list word you associate with each clue.

desiccated coconut __________
French Revolution __________
windsock __________
pollution __________
coloured lights __________
oxygen tanks __________
air traffic control __________
trucks __________
milk __________
jazz music __________
blindness __________
bats __________
swimming __________
shadow __________

2 Complete the table. In each full name, circle the letters used in the acronym.

acronym	full name
AWOL	
sonar	
	National Aeronautics and Space Administration
	Light amplification by stimulated emission of radiation
	Radio detection and ranging
PIN	
ASAP	

A **blend** is formed by joining parts of words together.
spelling + marathon → spellathon

3 Write the full words. Circle the letters that are used in the blend.

smog	______	brunch	______
heliport	______	blog	______
emoticon	______	electrocute	______
email	______	staycation	______

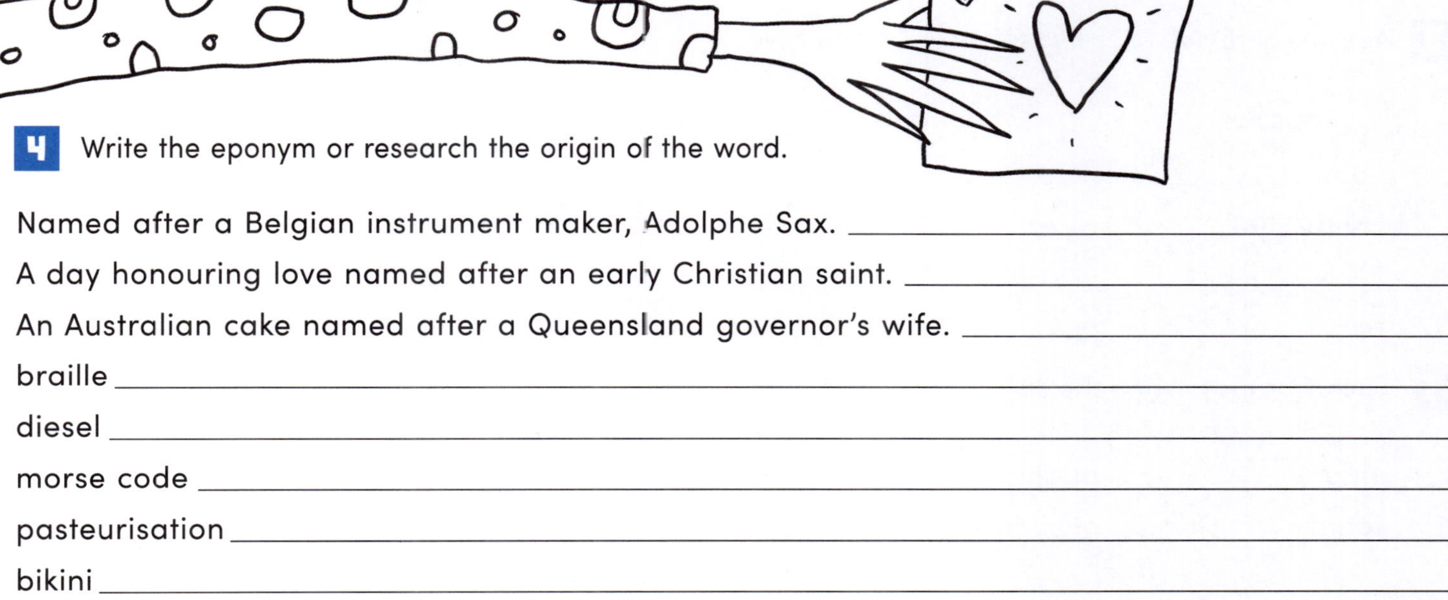

4 Write the eponym or research the origin of the word.

Named after a Belgian instrument maker, Adolphe Sax. ______

A day honouring love named after an early Christian saint. ______

An Australian cake named after a Queensland governor's wife. ______

braille ______

diesel ______

morse code ______

pasteurisation ______

bikini ______

Brand names sometimes become so well known that the name is used for similar products.

5 Write the original brand name that is now used to describe similar products.

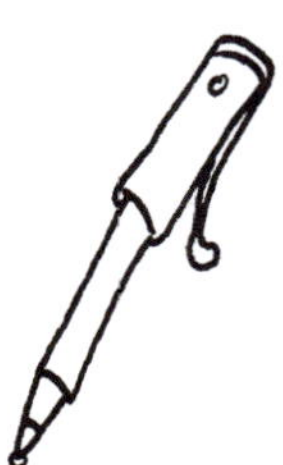

______ ______ ______ ______

Answer: a

Unit 12 Revision

What style of snowboarding makes it necessary to zigzag down a mountain?

a freestyle
b slalom
c cancan

1 Write the plural.

monarch	kidney	muscle	elbow
______	______	______	______
artery	bikini	iris	thigh
______	______	______	______

2 Add the suffix **al**, **ic** or **ous** to make an adjective.

virus	asthma	nerve	spine
______	______	______	______
contagion	gene	medicine	infection
______	______	______	______

3 Each word is missing the same sound. Add **c**, **ch** or **cc**.

s____eme	____ough	____emist	ex____ept	____riti____al
a____ident	____olesterol	____asualty	su____ess	me____ani____

4 One of the underlined consonants needs to be doubled and the other one doesn't. Write each word correctly. Use a dictionary if you need help.

ocasional ______	apendicitis ______
vacination ______	paralel ______
diarhoea ______	comunity ______
referal ______	acurate ______

5 Write whether each word is an acronym, abbreviation, blend or eponym. Explain the origin or write the full name for each term.

AIDS ______

flu ______

pasteurisation ______

polio ______

infotainment ______

Spelling Rules! Student Book 5 (ISBN 9780655092711) © Janelle Ho, Helen Pearson

6 Change each word to an adjective by adding **ible** or **able**.

rely	flex	change	adore	respect
sense	comfort	terror	value	misery

7 Many English words come from other languages. Write as many words as you can think of that originate from these Latin or Greek words.

Visio is Latin for *sight*.

Auditio is Latin for *hearing*.

Tele is Greek for *distance*.

Pedi is Latin for *foot.*

Novus is Latin for *new*.

---

8 All the double consonants have dropped out of this recount. Mark the consonants that need to be doubled. *recomend* (m marked with ^ after reco)

Today in asembly it was anounced that we would have no clases after lunch. Instead we would help our comunity by cleaning up the rubish along the river bank. Our teacher, Mr Patel, gave everyone a pair of ruber gloves and a bag, and we comenced work. I decided to work on the oposite bank where my eforts would be more obvious. Before long the bank was clean, so I steped into the mudy mangroves to continue. My feet imediately disapeared and I began to sink. I shouted to atract atention and almost the whole clas crosed the bridge to where I was. Some looked alarmed and some laughed and aplauded. Eventualy Mr Patel grabed me under each arm and lifted me onto the bank. I was shoeles and covered in mud. How embarasing!

Answer: b

Unit 13

Which game did English women invent because dribbling was too **aw**kward in long skirts?

a pie throwing
b hockey
c netball

Say Listen Look Understand Remember Practise

gawky ______
awkward ______
ordinary ______
organise ______
orphan ______
original ______
orchard ______
ornament ______
orthodontist ______
naughty ______
aural ______
audible ______
audition ______
exhaustion ______
authentic ______

1 Each word is missing the same sound. Add **aw**, **or** or **au**.

exh _ _ st	_ _ chard
squ _ _ k	n _ _ ghty
_ _ dinary	_ _ thority
d _ _ ghter	_ _ ganise
d _ _ n	n _ _ mal
_ _ kward	appl _ _ d

2 Write the list word that contains the smaller word.

name ______
hard ______
rig ______
war ______
us ______
hen ______
do ______
din ______

3 Match a base word and suffix to form a new word.

orphan	al	______
awe	ly	______
exhaust	age	______
ornament	some	______
authentic	ally	______
awkward	ion	______

4 Match a base word and prefix to form a new word.

extra	order	______
dis	ordinary	______
in	organic	______
non-	audible	______
dis	authentic	______
un	organised	______

5 Add suffixes to the base word to form word families.

ignore ______
______
explore ______
______

Spelling Rules! Student Book 5 (ISBN 9780655092711) © Janelle Ho, Helen Pearson

6 Use a dictionary to solve each clue.

1.	O	R										
2.	O	R										
3.	O	R										
4.	O	R										
5.	O	R										
6.	O	R										
7.	O	R										
8.	O	R										

1. either a part of your body or a musical instrument
2. a child who has no parents
3. grown without pesticide or other chemical additives
4. common
5. a group of musicians playing different instruments
6. used for decoration only
7. the scientific study of birds
8. a dentist who straightens teeth

7 Write the correct homophone.

pause paws pores pours

Whenever it rains the water ____________ into our back veranda.

The dog left the prints of its ____________ in the wet concrete.

Plants breathe through ____________ in their leaves.

Ali chattered on and on without needing to ____________ for breath.

Tip

The words **oral** and **aural** are often confused.
The word **oral** relates to speech or the mouth. It comes from the Latin word *oris*, meaning *mouth*.
The word **aural** relates to hearing or the ear. It comes from the Latin word *auris*, meaning *ear*.

8 Write the correct word.

Our school was fortunate to hear the ______________ histories from some Aboriginal Elders.

People with ______________ disabilities dance by feeling vibrations from the music.

Answer: c

Unit 14

What sport involves holding on to a heavy object, turning in a clockwise or **anti**clockwise direction, then throwing that object?

a hammer throwing
b spaniel tossing
c relay racing

Say **L**isten **L**ook **U**nderstand **R**emember **P**ractise

combine ______
companion ______
commemorate ______
comprehend ______
compel ______
conceal ______
concentrate ______
condescending ______
conference ______
consequence ______
antiseptic ______
antibiotic ______
anticlimax ______
antisocial ______
anticlockwise ______

Tip **com** is a prefix that means *together* or *with*. It can also intensify the meaning of the base word. **con** is a variant of **com**.

1 Add **com** or **con**.

____bine	____ceal	____nect
____plete	____pare	____ference
____sider	____pel	____pany
____mit	____bat	____sent

2 Use the words in question 1 and the list words to complete the rule.

Use **com** before base words beginning with ______.

Use **con** before base words beginning with ______.

3 Use a list word and its antonym to show the direction in which each creature moved.

The caterpillar crawled around the rim of the pot in an ______ direction.

The ant walked around the plate in a ______ direction.

What does **anti** mean? ______

4 Make medical words beginning with **anti**. Use a dictionary to write a definition for each word.

anti
- viral ______
- dote ______
- biotic ______
- septic ______

Spelling Rules! Student Book 5 (ISBN 9780655092711) © Janelle Ho, Helen Pearson

5 Write the list words in the correct column. Some words will appear in two columns.

adjective	verb	noun

6 Write a list word that is in the same word family.

company ____________________

anticlimactic ____________________

conferred ____________________

comprehension ____________________

concentration ____________________

concealment ____________________

7 Write a list word that contains a smaller word that matches each clue. Circle the smaller word.

a place to put your garbage in ____________________

order of events ____________________

an abbreviation for a month ____________________

?, twice, thrice ____________________

a note ____________________

? and key ____________________

a chicken that lays eggs ____________________

8 Write a story that ends in an anticlimax.

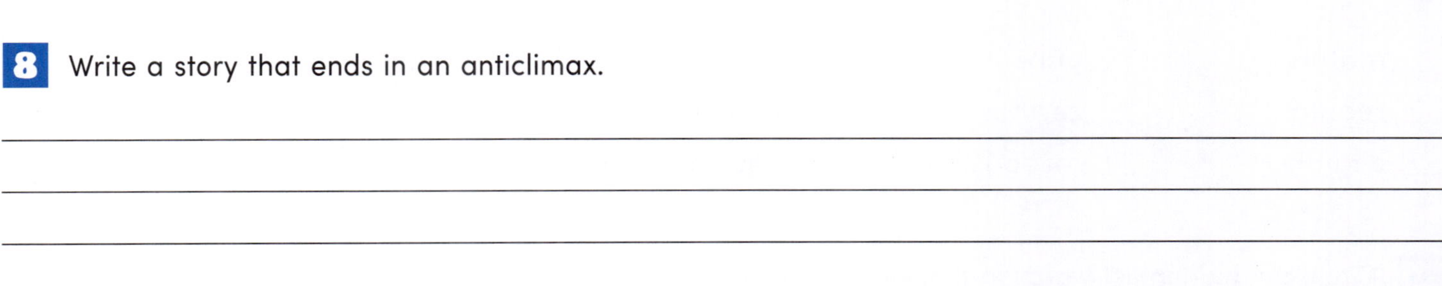

Answer: a

Unit 15

Which of these **im**practical-looking outfits was worn in the medieval sport of jousting?

a a tuxedo
b a suit of armour
c a Santa costume

Say Listen Look Understand Remember Practise

imperfect	____________
impatient	____________
impractical	____________
immature	____________
insane	____________
inappropriate	____________
inconvenient	____________
incapable	____________
indigestible	____________
irregular	____________
irrelevant	____________
irresponsible	____________
irresistible	____________
illegal	____________
illogical	____________

1 Each list word consists of a prefix + base word. Underline the base word in each list word. Colour the correct word in the sentence below.

Each base word is | an antonym | a synonym | of the list word.

Rule

The prefixes **in** and **un** can be used in front of base words beginning with most letters.
im is only used in front of **m** or **p**. *immortal* *impossible*
ir is only used in front of **r**. *irreversible*
il is only used in front of **l**. *illegible*

2 Make antonyms by adding **un**, **in**, **im**, **ir** or **il** as a prefix. Use a dictionary if you need help.

___mature	___pure	___direct	___logical	___proper
___regular	___certain	___legible	___rational	___sane
___eligible	___responsible	___capable	___proven	___legal

3 Circle the hidden list words in these sentences.

'I'm practically finished,' I told Mum proudly.

The archaeologist found a fossil leg, although it was badly damaged.

Our emergency kit contained safety pins, an elastic bandage and antiseptic cream.

'Come here! Ute's ill!' Ogi called urgently.

Amir regularly swims at the beach, even during winter.

'I'm Pati!' enthusiastically announced the new girl.

Spelling Rules! Student Book 5 (ISBN 9780655092711) © Janelle Ho, Helen Pearson

4 Circle the word that doesn't make sense in each sentence. Rewrite the sentence so it makes sense.

'Why did you leave your homework complete?' Mr De Silva inquired.

____

Terry was scolded for using appropriate language.

____

Our puppy coughed up a digestible piece of food.

____

An information report should include as much irrelevant information as impossible.

____

In gymnastics you score 10 out of 10 for an imperfect routine.

____

5 Tick the word if **im** or **in** is a prefix.

immortal	inactive
imagine	insecure
immune	insist
immigrant	inappropriate

6 These songs were recorded by bands whose names match the theme of the song. Use list words to complete the name of the song or the band.

Song	**Band**
'Still Totally Mad'	______________
'Still a Baby'	______________
'______________ Heartbeat'	Uneven Pulse
'Out of the Way'	______________

7 The words **illegal**, **eligible** and **illegible** are easily confused. Write the correct word in each sentence.

Anyone who donates at least $10 is ______________ to enter the lucky draw.

Gita committed a traffic offence by parking her car in an ______________ spot.

Mum was in such a rush this morning that her note is ______________.

Answer: b

Unit 16

Which **independent** racing birds can find their own way home?

a pigeons
b penguins
c dodos

Say **L**isten **L**ook **U**nderstand **R**emember **P**ractise

excellence ____________
undeserved ____________
reassuring ____________
irresponsibly ____________
unembarrassed ____________
knowledgeably ____________
acknowledgement ____________
imaginative ____________
dependable ____________
discontentment ____________
misfortunes ____________
inconveniently ____________
disastrously ____________
fascination ____________
misbehaviour ____________

1 Some list words are nouns. The number in the circle shows the number of prefixes and suffixes that have been added to the base word. Underline the base word and circle the prefixes and suffixes that have been added.

attendance (1)
ridiculousness (2)

dependable (1)
excellence (1)
fascination (1)
misbehaviour (2)
discontentment (2)
unembarrassed (2)
irresponsibly (3)

2 Use these prefix and suffix sums to make new words.

adverbs

sincere + ly = ____________
un + fortune + ate + ly = ____________
ir + regular + ly = ____________

adjectives

persuade + ive = ____________
in + depend + ent = ____________
ir + replace + able = ____________

3 Make a noun by adding the suffix. The base word changes in each case. Use a dictionary if you need help.

assume + tion = ____________
describe + tion = ____________
conclude + ion = ____________
deny + al = ____________
suspect + ion = ____________
social + ty = ____________

A word family consists of different words related to a base word.
Base word: *courage*
Related words: *encourage, discourage, encouragement, courageous, courageously*
Prefixes and suffixes added to the base word are types of **affixes**.

4 Write word families for these base words. Use one related word in a sentence.

appear ______________________________

____

believe ______________________________

____

sure ______________________________

____

5 Add one or more affixes to make a related word that completes each sentence.

The plumber apologised for the ______________ (convenient) it would cause when he turned off our water supply.

Mario felt ______________ (embarrass) when he tripped onto the stage.

The principal received a certificate ______________ (acknowledge) our efforts in Clean Up Australia Day.

Asha smiled ______________ (excite) as she was handed the trophy.

My parents are relieved to have copies of important documents after we had the ______________ (fortune) of being burgled.

Mum was taken aback by the ______________ (extravagant) of the gift.

6 Write a letter of apology for an April Fool's Day joke that went wrong. Use as many words as you can that contain prefixes and suffixes.

____

____

____

____

____

____

____

Answer: a

Unit 17

Different levels of **karate** are distinguished by the colour of which item of clothing?

a the underpants
b the cloak
c the belt

This week, the list words are on a map because English has adopted many words from other languages. Add your own words to the map.

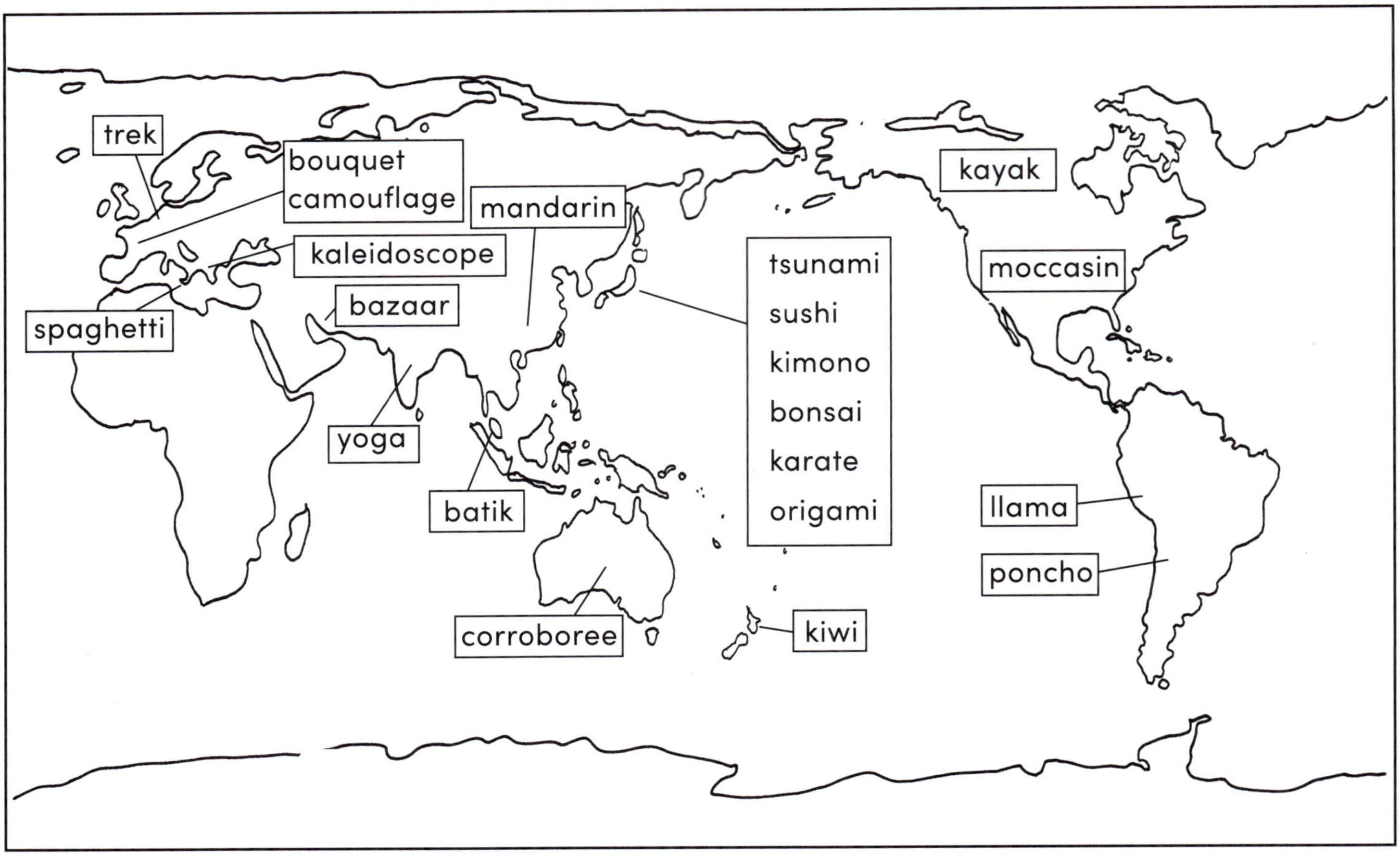

trek
bouquet
camouflage
mandarin
kaleidoscope
spaghetti
bazaar
yoga
batik
corroboree
tsunami
sushi
kimono
bonsai
karate
origami
kiwi
kayak
moccasin
llama
poncho

1 Write a list word that matches each definition and language.

word	definition	language
____________	physical and spiritual exercise	Hindi
____________	a bunch of flowers	French
____________	shoe made of soft leather	Algonquian (Native American)
____________	open-air market	Persian
____________	a method of printing on cloth	Malay
____________	destructive wave caused by an earthquake	Japanese
____________	closed canoe	Inuit (Canadian Eskimo)
____________	a journey on foot	Dutch
____________	a rectangle of cloth with a hole for the head	Araucanian (Chile)

Many food words come from Italian and French. Italian words often end in a vowel sound. French words often end in a silent consonant or silent **e**.

2 Group these food words according to their original language.

cappuccino champagne zucchini quiche calamari
camembert spaghetti crème brûlée broccoli nougat

French: ________________ Italian: ________________

________________ ________________ ________________ ________________

________________ ________________ ________________ ________________

3 Choose one of the Japanese words on the map to complete each sentence.

Luke loves eating ______________ but unfortunately he is allergic to soy sauce.

Successful ______________ requires skilful use of both roots and branches.

The pale colours of her ______________ contrasted with her shiny black hair.

I learn ______________ but my sister learns kung-fu.

Riyad enjoys craft so he borrowed a book on ______________.

4 These words are based on Indigenous names for Australian or New Zealand animals. Add **c**, **k** or **qu**.

___angaroo ___iwi ___ookaburra ___oll

___ea ___oala ___urrawong ___okka

5 The word element **scope** comes from the Greek *skopein*, which means *look at*. Write a word that ends in **scope** to match each clue.

Look through this to see a beautiful pattern. ______________

Astronomers say the bigger the better! ______________

Some things are too small to be seen without one. ______________

Every submarine has one. ______________

A doctor uses this to listen to your heart. ______________

6 *Mandarin* has three meanings: a fruit, a leader in ancient China and a language of northern China. Write a sentence for each meaning.

____

____

____

Answer: c

Unit 18 Revision

Which building did bungee jumper AJ Hackett leap off in front of **aw**estruck onlookers?

a the Eiffel Tower in France
b the Sky Tower Casino in New Zealand
c the shed in his backyard

1 Group these words as verbs or nouns, then complete the table. The first one has been done for you.

believe organisation dependence behave appear

verb	noun	antonym formed by adding a prefix
attend	attention	inattention

2 These sentences do not make sense. Rewrite them so they make sense, without using the word *not*.

The satisfied customer demanded to speak to the manager.

___

Vandalising public property is social behaviour.

___

Your story would be more interesting if you left out all the relevant information.

___

Kris celebrated the failure of her project.

___

The gallery paid a record sum for the fake Albert Namatjira painting.

___

3 These words need single or double consonants added. Write the words correctly using the consonants in brackets.

emba__a__ment (r, s) ___

di__a__ear (s, p) ___

ina__ro__riate (p, p) ___

i__ega__ (l, l) ___

co__e__orate (m, m) ___

co__o__oree (r, b) ___

4 Use the clues to find words you have learnt. Each word rhymes with the underlined word. The words in brackets give the meaning.

I argued my <u>cause</u> without ______________. (a break)

This book is <u>superb</u>, so please do not ______________ me. (interrupt)

Ms Jones apologised ______________ for having spoken so <u>severely</u>. (with clarity)

We were <u>forced</u> to repair the ______________ system on our car. (expulsion of gases)

Shari gave a ______________ as her <u>fork</u> fell to the floor. (harsh noise)

I will <u>devise</u> a way to ______________ myself so no one will recognise me! (conceal identity)

5 These words come from other languages. Draw a line to match each word to its origin.

llama	the French form of an Arabic word meaning kneeling place
mosquito	a French word for a table on which food is served
monsoon	a Spanish word meaning ittle fly
mosque	the Dutch form of an Arabic word meaning strong wind
tsunami	a Quechuan word for a relative of the camel
buffet	an Inuit word meaning house
igloo	a Japanese word meaning big wave

6 Not all the words with an **or** sound are correctly spelt. Circle the five mistakes. Then write the correct spelling of the words in the boxes.

In my imagination, I am a famous awthor. I see myself writing about noughty children who are always exploring and getting into awful mischief. Fautunately, they seem to be able to organise their way out of trouble as well as into it. The awsome adventures of my characters certainly do not reflect my oardinary and sometimes boring life!

7 Use a dictionary to find the meaning of this word. Write the meaning, then use the word in a sentence.

autobiographical ____

____

____

Answer: b

Unit 19

What aquatic sport involves aerobics in a swimming pool?

a aquatic tiddlywinks
b aquabotics
c aquarobics

Say Listen Look Understand Remember Practise	
aqua	______
liquid	______
frequent	______
quality	______
quantity	______
quiver	______
conquest	______
acquire	______
adequate	______
tranquil	______
eloquent	______
quotation	______
quarantine	______
inquisitive	______
acquaintance	______

1 Circle each syllable. Write the number of syllables in the box.

☐	aqua	☐	adequate
☐	queue	☐	tranquil
☐	frequent	☐	quarantine
☐	liquid	☐	acquaintance

squash

2 Add the missing vowels to make a list word.

c _ nq _ _ st	tr _ nq _ _ l
q _ _ v _ r	l _ q _ _ d
_ q _ _	_ l _ q _ _ nt
q _ _ nt _ ty	q _ _ l _ ty
_ cq _ _ r _	_ d _ q _ _ t _

3 Write a list word that is a synonym.

tremble	amount	calm	curious
______	______	______	______
sufficient	obtain	triumph	well-spoken
______	______	______	______
often	fluid	isolation	contact
______	______	______	______

The **a** in *squat* and *qualify* does not make its usual short vowel sound. Instead, it sounds like a short **o**. Some common words where **a** makes the short **o** sound are *was, what, want, watch, wash.*

4 Write three list words in which **a** makes the short **o** sound.

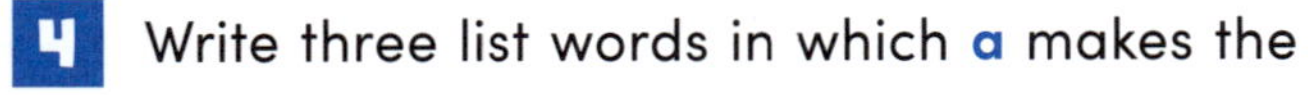

______ ______ ______

Spelling Rules! Student Book 5 (ISBN 9780655092711) © Janelle Ho, Helen Pearson

5 Write **qu** words.

It was so ______________ sitting on the beach watching the moon rise.

______________ officers check all animal and agricultural products arriving in Australia.

You must take ______________ supplies of water if you are travelling in the desert.

I was surprised by the large ______________ of sugar you ______________ to make jam.

The ______________ to ______________ free entry tickets was extremely long.

6 Complete the puzzle. Use a dictionary if you need help.

1.	Q	U	I									
2.	Q	U	I									
3.	Q	U	A									
4.	Q	U	A									
5.	Q	U	O									
6.	Q	U	O									
7.	Q	U	E									
8.	Q	U	I									
9.	Q	U	E									

1. give up
2. sssh!
3. a colourless rock
4. a dispute
5. the answer when you divide two numbers
6. use of someone else's spoken or written words
7. an Australian state
8. five babies born at the same time
9. of doubtful quality

7 *Aqua* is the Latin word for water. Write as many words as you can that begin with *aqua*. Use a dictionary if you need help.

____

____

8 Use a dictionary to find the meaning of the words elo**qu**ent and lo**qu**acious. Write the meanings, then use each word in a sentence.

eloquent ____

____

____

loquacious ____

____

____

The root word is *loqui*, which is Latin for ______________.

Answer: c

Unit 20

Polo is usually played on horseback. What other animal plays in a unique version of the game?

a emu
b elephant
c piglet

Say Listen Look Understand Remember Practise	
tongue	______
rogue	______
plague	______
colleague	______
fatigue	______
intrigue	______
dialogue	______
catalogue	______
synagogue	______
unique	______
antique	______
technique	______
boutique	______
mosque	______
plaque	______

1 Use each clue to find a smaller word inside a list word. Write the list word, underlining the smaller word that matches the clue.

clue	list word
opposite of in	boutique
pester	______
a common pet	______
insect	______
opposite of off	______
opposite of thin	______
what 'L' in AFL and NRL stands for	______
? a phone number	______

2 Rewrite each sentence without changing its meaning by including a list word.

I knew where to find the book because I had looked in the list of books available in the library.

______

Tiredness can be a problem when you are travelling long distances.

______

Brodie's science teacher demonstrated a safe way to mix the chemicals.

______

My cousin invited many of the people she works with to her wedding.

______

Internet offers are regularly posted by tricksters.

______

Many Australian animals are not found anywhere else in the world.

______

3 Choose the correct words to complete the table.

church rabbi mosque imam synagogue priest

religion	place of worship	leader
Judaism	______	______
Islam	______	______
Christianity	______	______

4 **Uni**, **bi** and **tri** are from Latin words meaning one, two and three. Use a dictionary to find words beginning with **uni**, **bi** and **tri**.

uni ______

bi ______

tri ______

5 Write the meaning of each word. Then write the correct word to complete each sentence.

plaque: ______

plague: ______

The barley crop was ruined by a ______ of locusts.

Using dental floss regularly helps reduce ______ and tooth decay.

A brass ______ marks the spot where the time capsule is buried.

6 Add a list word to fit each category.

scoundrel	knave	rascal	______
tiredness	weariness	lethargy	______
conversation	debate	discussion	______
ancient	historical	second-hand	______
lips	gum	teeth	______

7 Write about a uni**que** experience. Use as many list words and other words with **qu** as you can.

______

______

______

______

______

______

Answer: b

Unit 21

Kabaddi is a game of team pursuit played in some Asian countries. What must the players chant throughout the game?

a Kabaddi, kabaddi!
b Kabaddi, come here!
c Eeny, meeny, miny moe

Say Listen Look Understand Remember Practise

fluid ____
ruin ____
suitcase ____
guide ____
guilty ____
biscuit ____
pursuit ____
suitable ____
guitar ____
inquire ____
bruise ____
intuition ____
nuisance ____
mosquito ____
circuit ____

1 ui usually makes a single vowel sound. However, in three list words, the u and i belong to different syllables. Write the three words.

____
____
____

Tip As a single vowel sound, ui can be pronounced different ways, for example short i as in guilty, long oo as in suit, long i as in guide.

2 Write list words where ui makes the long oo sound.

____ ____
____ ____

Rule If a word ends in silent e, drop the e when adding y to make an adjective.

3 Make an adjective by adding y.

fruit ____ juice ____ sugar ____ crumble ____ ice ____

4 Add affixes to make new words. Use the new words in a sentence.

un + suit + able ____

____

inquire + y + es ____

____

5 Write compound words to match each picture.

 ____

____

____

Spelling Rules! Student Book 5 (ISBN 9780655092711) © Janelle Ho, Helen Pearson

6 Add **cui** or **gui** to make a word.

pen____n	dis____se	cir____t
____dance	mis____ded	____sine
bis____t	____tarist	____llotine

Tip **Sweet** and **suite** are homophones. **Suit** and **suite** are often confused.

7 Write the correct word from the tip to complete each sentence.

Mum was furious when I spilt hot chocolate on the new lounge ______________.

On Father's Day I gave Dad a tie to match his new ______________.

My favourite meal is ______________ and sour chicken.

In a deck of cards, hearts is a red ______________.

8 Make words ending with **ition**. Match each word to its definition.

ition: intu, premon, appar, amb, inhib, dispos

______________ a feeling of shyness

______________ ability to grasp the truth without evidence

______________ a desire to do well

______________ a forewarning

______________ a ghost or phantom

______________ nature or temperament

Tip These pairs are homophones:

- **crews** and **cruise**
- **sweet** and **suite**.

This pair is often confused: **suit** and **suite**.

9 Write sentences using each pair of homophones. You can add any affix you need.

____

____

____

____

____

Answer: a

Unit 22

What annual yacht race starts in a harbour on Boxing Day?

a The Paris to Dakar
b The Sydney to Hobart
c The Melbourne Cup

Say Listen Look Understand Remember Practise	
flour	______
course	______
flavour	______
favourite	______
colourful	______
humour	______
harbour	______
journal	______
nourish	______
honour	______
odour	______
mournful	______
detour	______
behaviour	______
tournament	______

1 Add the missing consonant to these words ending in **our**.

fla __ our	co __ our
vi __ our	va __ our
har __ our	ho __ our
o __ our	hu __ our
de __ our	fa __ our
beha __ iour	sa __ iour

2 Write a list word that rhymes.

source	flourish
______	______
savour	kernel
______	______
folder	power
______	______
scornful	barber
______	______

3 Complete each word by adding **or** or **our**.

There's a nasty od___ out in the corrid___!

Lemons have a pleasant flav___ but they are very s___.

The police inspect___ has kept a j___nal for over thirty years.

A customer dropped a bag of fl___ on the escalat___. What a mess!

We all stood to hon___ the arrival of the govern___.

Divers found an anch___ from a 19th century shipwreck at the bottom of the harb___.

4 Write these numbers as words.

37 = *thirty-seven*

14 ______

48 ______

104 ______

444 ______

5 Write the homophone or homophones. Then choose the correct spelling to complete the sentence.

source ____________ I like vanilla ice-cream served with chocolate ____________.

course ____________ Of ____________ she likes birthday parties!

flour ____________ Make bread dough with ____________, water and yeast.

mourning ____________ Black is the traditional colour of ____________.

your ____________ Watch where ____________ going!

Remember to put ____________ name on your jacket.

pour ____________ I like to ____________ over joke books.

____________ Ouch! My dog has a thorn in his ____________.

Tip **our** and **hour** are homophones. **our** and **are** are not!

6 Fill in **our**, **hour** or **are**.

We ________ still an ________ away from ________ house because we have to make a detour to the harbour.

7 Make words starting with *tour*. Use each word in a sentence.

tour – ist ____

tour – nament ____

tour – niquet ____

Tip Some words are spelt differently in Australian and American English. When you use a computer spellchecker, make sure you have the language set to Australian English.

8 Draw a wriggly red line under the words that are spelt incorrectly in Australian English. Write the words correctly.

Uncle Bob is my favorite relative, so I'm always on my best behavior. He has a wicked sense of humor and always wears crazy, colorful clothes. Whenever I can, I go sailing with him on Sydney Harbor. He calls me 'Able Seaman' and I call him 'Honorable Cap'n'. Sometimes after we finish sailing, we buy gelato at the shop near the wharf. Uncle Bob always gets caramel because he loves that flavor.

____
____
____
____
____
____
____

Answer: b

Unit 23

Which sport was once **popular** in Britain, but is now illegal?

a pig flinging
b rubber ducky shooting
c fox hunting

Say Listen Look Understand Remember Practise	
popular	______________
manual	______________
library	______________
inhabit	______________
universe	______________
delicate	______________
circular	______________
equator	______________
benefit	______________
democracy	______________
dependent	______________
monotonous	______________
microscope	______________
magnificent	______________
contradict	______________

1 Write the list word that is derived from the Latin or Greek word. Use a dictionary to find two more words with the same origin.

Latin

liber = book ______________
______________ ______________

inhabitare = dwell ______________
______________ ______________

manus = hand ______________
______________ ______________

Greek

demos = people ______________
______________ ______________

mikros = small ______________
______________ ______________

2 Write the missing letters, using the definition as a clue.

deli __ __ __ __	fine or dainty	bene __ __ __	an advantage
deli __ __ __ __ __	pleasing in taste	bene __ __ __ __ __ __	helpful
deli __ __ __	pleasure	benev __ __ __ __ __	kindly
equa __ __ __	midway between North and South Poles	popul __ __	liked by many people
equa __ __ __ __	to make equal	popul __ __ __ __ __	people who live in a town, city or country
equi __ __ __	equal day and night	popul __ __ __ __ __	to make popular
circu __ __ __	shaped like a circle	depend __ __ __	relying on another for support
circu __ __	a track that ends up where it started	depend __ __ __ __	able to be relied upon
circum __ __ __ ence	outside edge of a circle	__ __dependent	able to stand alone

Spelling Rules! Student Book 5 (ISBN 9780655092711)

3 Make words using the endings in the box. Write a definition for each word.

–dict –tonous –fy –logue –ry –ficent

magni________ ______________________________

magni________ ______________________________

contra________ ______________________________

contra________ ______________________________

mono________ ______________________________

mono________ ______________________________

4 These word elements come from Latin (L) and Greek (G) words. Write as many related words as you can.

meter = measure (G) ______________________________

semi = half (G) ______________________________

quad = four (L) ______________________________

oct = eight (L) ______________________________

multi = many (L) ______________________________

poly = many (G) ______________________________

5 Say each word aloud. Underline the stressed syllable.

popular	inhabitable	library	monotone	meter
unpopular	uninhabitable	librarian	monotonous	diameter

6 Circle the word in the sentence that does not make sense. Rewrite each sentence so it makes sense.

Astronomers use radio and optical microscopes.

____

Be careful of the sharp corners on the circular table.

____

We won the debate because our arguments were persuasive and contradictory.

____

Answer: c

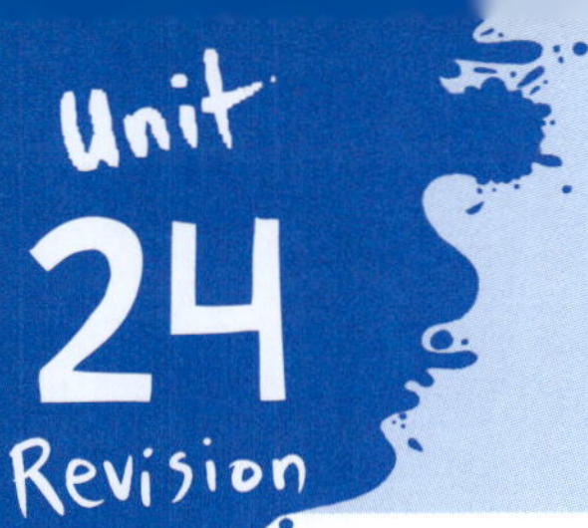

What do you do in the game of squash?

a squeeze as many people as possible into a phone booth
b hit a small rubber ball inside a walled court
c make orange juice

1 Complete the tables.

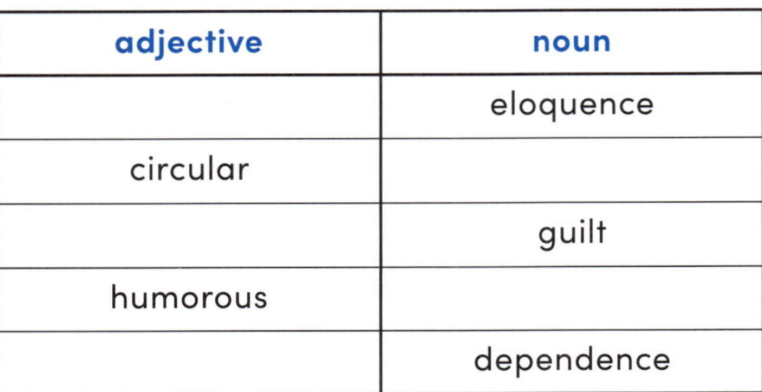

adjective	noun
	eloquence
circular	
	guilt
humorous	
	dependence

adjective	verb
	magnify
mournful	
	honour
intriguing	
	favour

2 Use alliteration to complete each sentence.

Fran ________________ flies to France.

Roger rapidly realised that his ________________ was unreasonable.

Dad's ________________ has a collection of curious coins.

The TV program on poisonous parasites was very ________________.

Tan won a trophy at the tennis ________________.

3 Some phrases are not meant literally. Write a sentence to show the meaning of each expression.

tongue in cheek

____

slip of the tongue

____

tongue-twister

____

forked tongue

____

mother tongue

____

Spelling Rules! Student Book 5 (ISBN 9780655092711) © Janelle Ho, Helen Pearson

4 Most of the vowels have been left out of these sentences. Write each sentence correctly.

If my fvrt bscts were nt so pplr, I wld gt to eat mny more!

____

Many cntrs cls to the eqtr unfrtntly sffr frm disses csed by msqto.

____

The hvy stcse I tk on our hldy was a nsnce.

____

The scentst usd an intrgng nw tchnq n hs xprmnt.

____

5 Complete the puzzle. Use the definitions and the Latin words in brackets as clues.

Across

1. rule expressed in symbols (*form*)
6. place to suntan in artificial light (*solaris*)
9. tank for fish (*aqua*)
10. person who relies on someone (*dependere*)
12. state or condition (*qualitas*)
13. joined together (*uni*)

Down

2. very old (*antiquus*)
3. funny (*humor*)
4. number of people (*popularis*)
5. works by hand (*manus*)
7. someone who walks (*pedi*)
8. special importance (*honor*)
11. able to be carried (*portare*)

Answer: b

Unit 25

Which insect **emits** its own light?

a a glow worm
b a dragonfly
c a ladybug

Say **L**isten **L**ook **U**nderstand **R**emember **P**ractise	
admit	______
permit	______
submit	______
emit	______
impress	______
compress	______
repress	______
suppress	______
offer	______
refer	______
prefer	______
infer	______
confer	______
suffer	______
transfer	______

1 The Latin root word *mittere* means *to send* or *let go*. Make list words with different prefixes.

ex + mittere ______
ad + mittere ______
per + mittere ______
sub + mittere ______

2 Use the definition to write the meaning of the prefix.

emit: give forth or send forth
ex-: ______
admit: let enter; acknowledge a crime or mistake
ad-: ______
permit: allow or let through
per-: ______
submit: place under the control of someone or something
sub-: ______

3 Write a list word or a related word. Then write its definition.

in- (into or upon) + premere (press or cover) ______

______

com- (with or together) + premere (press or cover) ______

______

re- (back) + premere (press or cover) ______

______

sub- (under) + premere (press or cover) ______

______

ex- (out) + premere (press or cover) ______

______

de- (down) + premere (press or cover) ______

______

Spelling Rules! Student Book 5 (ISBN 9780655092711) © Janelle Ho, Helen Pearson

4 Use an etymological dictionary to find the parts of each word. Write each part and its meaning.

refer: ______________________ + ______________________

prefer: ______________________ + ______________________

suffer: ______________________ + ______________________

offer: ______________________ + ______________________

infer: ______________________ + ______________________

transfer: ______________________ + ______________________

confer: ______________________ + ______________________

5 Make words using the prefix. Check a dictionary to make sure that the word part is a prefix.

pre-: ____

trans-: ____

ex-: ____

6 Four list words are both verbs and nouns. Write the words.

______________ ______________ ______________ ______________

7 Write a list word to complete the expression.

______________ a reward

______________ a mistake

______________ with your teammate

______________ in silence

______________ a cough

______________ an assignment

______________ the judge

______________ a light

8 Write about a time when something or someone impressed you.

____

____

____

____

____

____

____

____

____

____

____

Answer: a

Unit 26

What do the five rings of the Olympic Games symbolise?

a the number of hoops a poodle can jump through
b the number of gold medals won at the first Olympic Games
c the different continents of the world

Say Listen Look Understand Remember Practise	
type	______
byte	______
rhyme	______
myth	______
gypsy	______
rhythm	______
oxygen	______
symbol	______
synthetic	______
typical	______
pyjamas	______
physician	______
sympathy	______
century	______
tragedy	______

Tip y can make either a short or long i sound.

1 Write i or y.

b __ c __ cle
g __ mnastics
ox __ gen
p __ gst __
h __ stor __ c
p __ jamas
m __ th
g __ ps __
l __ brar __
m __ ster __
t __ p __ cal
sat __ sf __
s __ mpath __
rh __ thm

2 Group these fabrics.

nylon	silk	cotton	rayon
corduroy	wool	polyester	felt

Made from natural fibres

____

Made from synthetic fibres

____

Tip In words of Greek origin, ph sounds like f.

3 Write the missing letters, using the definition as a clue.

P	H	Y					scientific study of matter and motion							
P	H	Y						relating to the body						
P	H	A						a place to get medicines						
P	H	Y							a doctor					
P	H	I								study of truth and knowledge				
P	H	O									the use of a camera to make images			
P	H	O												the making of nutrients by plants

c makes an s sound when it is followed by y.

4 Write c or s to complete each word. Write a definition for each one.

__ystem ________________

__ynonym ________________

__yclone ________________

__ymphony ________________

__ymmetry ________________

__yllable ________________

__ylinder ________________

__ympathy ________________

__yberspace ________________

__ygnet ________________

5 Write the correct homophone in each space.

The percussionist's music used a ____________ to indicate when the ____________ should sound. (cymbal, symbol)

I thought the octopus was about to ____________ when I saw it squirt black ____________ into the water. (die, dye)

When I cooked the beef stew this ____________, I remembered to add ____________. (time, thyme)

6 Computer memory is measured in bytes. Write what each computer abbreviation stands for and how many bytes it represents.

MB ____________ GB ____________ TB ____________

7 Write the appropriate word in each space.

rapidly tiny paralyses century deadly tragedy oxygen

____________ blue-ringed octopuses are ____________ to humans. Their sting ____________ the victim's muscles. This means the victim can't breathe and will ____________ die from lack of ____________. Fortunately in the 21st ____________, medical assistance can sometimes avert this ____________.

Answer: c

Unit 27

981 people in New Zealand displayed their sporting creativity when they ran in a race wearing what item of clothing?

a cowboy hats
b Wellington boots
c wedding dresses

Say Listen Look Understand Remember Practise

variety	______
poverty	______
charity	______
creativity	______
simplicity	______
sincerity	______
personality	______
maturity	______
majority	______
minority	______
electricity	______
familiarity	______
speciality	______
opportunity	______
authority	______

1 Colour the correct word.

The list words are all

nouns	verbs	adjectives	adverbs

2 Write the list words that have the form base word + ity without any changes.

list word	base word
______	______
______	______
______	______
______	______
______	______
______	______

3 Write the list words that have base words ending in **e**.

list word	base word
______	______
______	______
______	______
______	______
______	______

4 Use the clues to find a smaller word inside a list word. Write the list word and underline the smaller word that matches the clue. Try not to use the same word twice.

clue	list word
person who writes books	<u>author</u>ity
person who does not tell the truth	______
floor rug	______
boy child of parents	______
consume	______
large urban area	______
opposite of under	______
place where ships dock	______
vote for someone	______
partially burn	______

Spelling Rules! Student Book 5 (ISBN 9780655092711) © Janelle Ho, Helen Pearson

5 Complete these sayings. All the words end in **ty**, but not all are list words.

______________ killed the cat.

______________ is the spice of life.

______________ begins at home.

______________ is the mother of invention.

______________ breeds contempt.

6 Colour the correct word.

Tom apologised, but his words lacked [sincerity | insincerity].

Showing off is often a sign of [maturity | immaturity].

I enjoy sport, so I was disappointed that the [majority | minority] of my friends wanted to watch a movie.

Research has shown that education is a path out of [prosperity | poverty].

Boost your health by eating a [variety | monotony] of fresh vegetables.

The [simplicity | complexity] of the machine makes it difficult to repair.

7 Make a noun ending in **ty** that belongs to the same word family. Use the noun in a sentence.

active ______________________________

____________ ______________________________

safe ______________________________

____________ ______________________________

cruel ______________________________

____________ ______________________________

immune ______________________________

____________ ______________________________

8 Add vowels to make nouns ending in **ity**. Write a synonym.

n__c__ss__ty ______________________

__b__l__ty ______________________

c__mm__n__ty ______________________

pr__ __r__ty ______________________

__t__rn__ty ______________________

s__m__l__r__ty ______________________

p__p__l__r__ty ______________________

__ct__v__ty ______________________

s__c__r__ty ______________________

c__mpl__x__ty ______________________

Answer: b

Unit 28

What was Golden Flame, the brilliant athlete who broke a high-jumping record when it jumped 46 centimetres?

a a chimpanzee
b a rabbit
c a flea

Say **L**isten **L**ook **U**nderstand **R**emember **P**ractise

brilli**ant**	____________
ignor**ant**	____________
domin**ant**	____________
toler**ant**	____________
hesit**ant**	____________
depend**ant**	____________
redund**ant**	____________
obedi**ent**	____________
consist**ent**	____________
incid**ent**	____________
perman**ent**	____________
suffici**ent**	____________
effici**ent**	____________
coher**ent**	____________
immin**ent**	____________

1 Complete each word by adding **ent** or **ant**.

differ_____	brilli_____
hesit_____	excell_____
dist_____	magnific_____
confid_____	conveni_____
ignor_____	toler_____
consist_____	extravag_____
reluct_____	frequ_____

2 Make an antonym by adding **un**, **in** or **dis**.

____tolerant	____important
____sufficient	____obedient
____efficient	____consistent
____frequent	____convenient

3 Write two list words that can be used as nouns.

_ _ _ _ _ _ _ _

_ _ _ _ _ _ _ _ _

Tip

The word **dependent** is an adjective. It means reliant or depending on.
Many chicks are completely dependent on their parents for food.
The word **dependant** is a noun. It means a person who depends on someone else.
Mr and Mrs Dean have two dependants, both aged under twelve.

4 Write whether the underlined word is an adjective or a noun. Then write your own sentence for each usage.

How healthy you are is <u>dependent</u> on diet and exercise. ____________

The government will give each <u>dependant</u> $200. ____________

dependent: ____

____

dependant: ____

____

5 Write the list word that could replace the underlined word or words in each sentence.

Dad rushed to the shops because we didn't have enough candles for Grandma's birthday cake.

____

Don't use that pen on the board! It makes marks that are always there. ________________

The new student was not confident about entering the classroom. ________________

To be persuasive, your arguments must be logically consistent. ________________

Tip People sometimes use unnecessary words. For example, you do not need to describe a result as *very excellent*, because *excellent* already tells you the result is superb. The unnecessary words are redundant.

6 Cross out the redundant words in each sentence.

Each person's fingerprints are very unique.

The imminent storm is coming very soon.

The lawyer labelled the document 'Very Urgent.'

We used a bucket for a letterbox until Mum built a permanent one that would last.

Very Urgent

7 Colour the correct homophone.

Harry's [current | currant] swimming coach once represented Australia.

If you don't insert the batteries correctly, the electricity [current | currant] cannot flow.

The fruit cake contained [currents | currants] as well as sultanas and raisins.

The river flowed smoothly, with a swift [current | currant].

8 Write words ending in **ant** or **ent**.

Dear Inspector,

I am writing to you about a curious ________________ that occurred last Thursday night. I feel that it is ________________ that you know about it, though I was initially ________________ to contact you, in case my report was doubted.

Last Thursday evening, a ________________ flash in the night sky alerted me to the presence of an alien spaceship. The spaceship's rockets have left ________________ marks in the grass of my backyard, where it landed.

I feel that this matter requires ________________ investigation. I am ________________ that you will undertake such an inquiry in an ________________ manner.

Yours sincerely,

Mar Shen

Answer: b

Unit 29

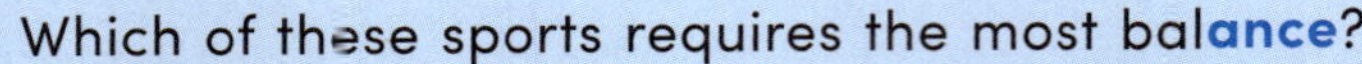

Which of these sports requires the most bal**ance**?

a orienteering
b crumpet eating
c rollerblading

Say Listen Look Understand Remember Practise

dist**ance** ____________
bal**ance** ____________
assist**ance** ____________
resist**ance** ____________
signific**ance** ____________
reluct**ance** ____________
insur**ance** ____________
surveill**ance** ____________
mainten**ance** ____________
influ**ence** ____________
experi**ence** ____________
viol**ence** ____________
exist**ence** ____________
evid**ence** ____________
consci**ence** ____________

Tip If the adjective ends in **ent**, the noun usually ends in **ence**.
If the adjective ends in **ant**, the noun usually ends in **ance**.

1 Complete the table.

adjective	noun
violent	
	significance
resistant	
	absence
tolerant	
	magnificence
evident	
	ignorance
distant	

2 The number in the circle is the number of syllables in the complete word. Use this information to help you work out the ending for each noun.

audi__________ (3)
buoy__________ (3)
experi__________ (4)
urg__________ (3)
effici__________ (4)
bal__________ (2)
frequ__________ (3)
reluct__________ (3)

Tip Some nouns end in **ency** or **ancy**.

3 Write a list word to complete the sentence.

To reduce crime, the shopping centre installed ____________ cameras.

It is customary for the Speaker of the House to show great ____________ and have to be dragged to the seat of honour.

The car might have been cheap to buy but its ____________ was expensive!

The ____________ of the yeti has never been verified.

Spelling Rules! Student Book 5 (ISBN 9780655092711) © Janelle Ho, Helen Pearson

4 The words *influence* and *experience* can be a noun or a verb. Write which one it is. Then write a sentence using it a different way.

The weather is known to influence a person's mood. ______________

Your sentence: ____

____

I hope seeing dolphins swim in the ocean will not be a once-in-a-lifetime experience. ______________

Your sentence: ____

____

Tip

Sometimes people confuse **conscience** with **conscious**.
Conscience (a noun) = the internal faculty that tells right from wrong
Conscious (an adjective) = aware

5 Use each word in a sentence.

conscience	____
	____
conscious	____
	____

6 Complete the puzzle. Each clue is a noun and the solution is a verb. Both words belong to the same word family.

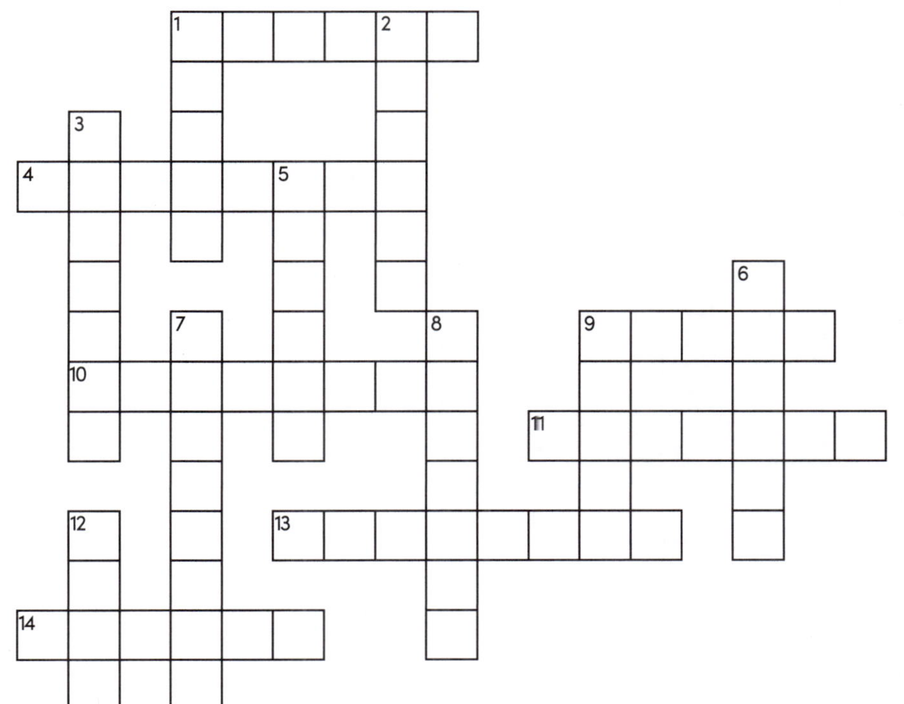

Across

1. appearance
4. hesitancy
9. excellence
10. reassurance
11. significance
13. tolerance
14. resistance

Down

1. avoidance
2. attendance
3. performance
5. assistance
6. residence
7. maintenance
8. neglectfulness
9. existence
12. obedience

Answer: c

Unit 30 Revision

What is the longest distance travelled in one hour on a unicycle?

a 10.65 kilometres
b right along the Great Wall of China
c 3000 kilometres

1 Write the number of syllables in the circle. Underline the stressed syllable.

irresponsibly ◯	fatigue ◯	preference ◯	consequence ◯
imminent ◯	archaeology ◯	analyses ◯	corroboree ◯

2 Write the plural.

storey ____________

democracy ____________

fungus ____________

arch ____________

fiasco ____________

3 Complete the table.

word	add **ed**	add **ing**
deny		
annoy		
balance		
suffer		
permit		

4 Write the most common grammatical class for each suffix.

-ed ____________

-able ____________

-ity ____________

-ly ____________

-ent ____________ ____________

5 Write a word ending in **ent** or **ant** to match each clue.

1.	U				N	T		
2.	C					N	T	
3.	V					N	T	
4.	H						N	T
5.	R							N	T
6.	P							N	T

1. needing immediate action
2. happening now
3. antonym of gentle
4. unsure whether to act
5. synonym for unwilling
6. antonym of temporary

6 Change the circled letter to make a new word. Write R after the pairs that rhyme.

(r)elay ____________	(r)oyal ____________	s(t)ay ____________
(h)ype ____________	pr(a)y ____________	curr(a)nt ____________
disma(l) ____________	m(o)th ____________	t(o)pical ____________

Spelling Rules! Student Book 5 (ISBN 9780655092711) © Janelle Ho, Helen Pearson

7 Write as many words as you can that belong to each word family. Use prefixes, suffixes and different word classes to add to your list.

sign: signify, signifies, signified, signifying, significant, insignificant, significance, insignificance, significantly

assist: ______________________________

____

obey: ______________________________

____

special: ______________________________

____

8 Use the clues to make a word.

var [eye] ety ______________

op [pour] tunity ______________

su [fish] ent ______________

curio [city] ______________

consis [tent] ______________

main10ance ______________

9 Proofread this text. The text has six words that are incorrect. Circle the mistakes. Then write the correct spelling of the words in the boxes.

Yuki loves circuses. She laughs louder than anyone else in the audiance when the clowns perform. She holds her breathe during the trapeze act, hoping that no dangerous incident will occur. The last time she went to a circus, there was a display of gypsy dancing. The women wore colorful dresses that swirled to the rhythem of the music as the men wove complex patterns between them. What a magnificant sight! Yuki wants the circus to come back to her town soon, so she can experience the many magicle moments all over again.

Answer: a

Unit 31

Who was worshipped by the Ancient Roman people as the god of wrestling and gymnastics?

a Lady Gaga

b Mercury

c Pocahontas

Say Listen Look Understand Remember Practise

machinery	________
schedule	________
tissue	________
tension	________
ferocious	________
suspicious	________
appreciate	________
luscious	________
commercial	________
initiate	________
confidential	________
influential	________
complexion	________
ambitious	________
conscientious	________

Tip sh rarely comes in the middle of a base word.

1 Sort the words into two groups depending on whether sh is in the middle or at the end of the base word.

fashion	squashing	cashew
splashed	hairbrushes	worship
fleshy	nourishment	cushion

sh in middle of base word

________ ________

________ ________

sh at end of base word

________ ________

________ ________

____

Tip There are many ways to write the sh sound: s, sh, ch, sch, si, ci, ti, ss and sci.

2 Write the sh sound for each word. The words in each group use the same letter pattern.

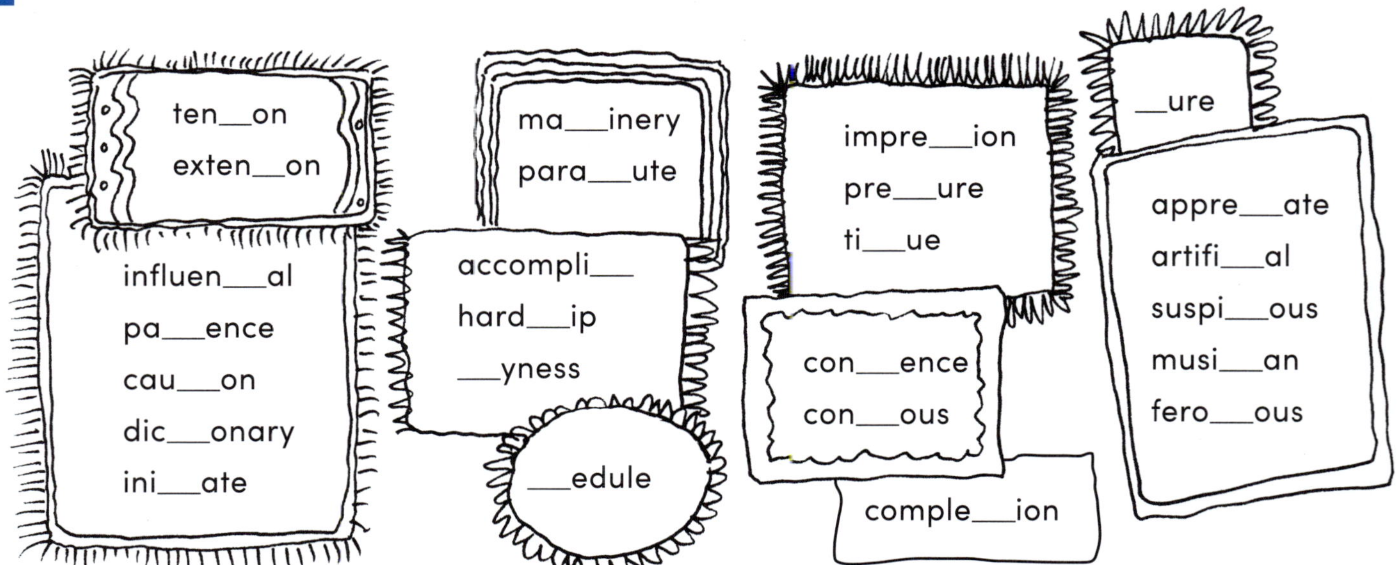

ten__on
exten__on

ma__inery
para__ute

impre__ion
pre__ure
ti__ue

__ure

influen__al
pa__ence
cau__on
dic__onary
ini__ate

accompli__
hard__ip
__yness

__edule

con__ence
con__ous

comple__ion

appre__ate
artifi__al
suspi__ous
musi__an
fero__ous

Spelling Rules! Student Book 5 (ISBN 9780655092711) © Janelle Ho, Helen Pearson

Words with **ch** that have the **sh** sound are often originally French.

3 Use the meanings to write a word where **ch** sounds like **sh** and is French in origin.

__________________ cook

__________________ driver

__________________ information booklet

__________________ device to slow a person falling through the air

__________________ unshaved hair above the mouth

4 These words are pronounced differently in Australian and American English. Say each word both ways. Which pronunciation is used in each country?

schedule ceremony lieutenant laboratory aluminium herb

5 Use the clues to write adjectives ending in **tial** or **cial**. Write the hidden word.

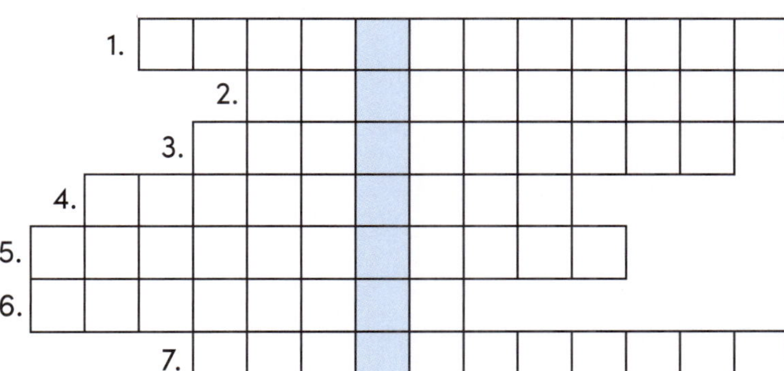

1. in confidence
2. of benefit
3. not natural; not real
4. absolutely necessary
5. on the surface; not deep
6. with the authority of a particular office
7. having influence

Hidden word: ____________________

6 Use the clues to write adjectives ending in **tious** or **cious**. Write the hidden word.

1. bad or violent
2. having ambition
3. of great value
4. believing in the supernatural
5. acting according to conscience
6. fierce
7. food that is good for you is…
8. having suspicion

Hidden word: ____________________

Answer: b

Unit 32

Which of these foods is not eaten in an eating contest?
a pretzels
b hamburgers
c muesli

Say **L**isten **L**ook **U**nderstand **R**emember **P**ractise

noodle ______
hamburger ______
schnitzel ______
strudel ______
muesli ______
pretzel ______
delicatessen ______
kindergarten ______
abseil ______
blitz ______
rucksack ______
wanderlust ______
uber ______
kaput ______
waltz ______

1 Write list words.

Food: ______ ______ ______ ______ ______ ______

Places: ______ ______

Music: ______

Adventure: ______ ______

Tip **sch** and **tz** are common letter patterns in German words.

2 Write list words. Then write another word.

	list word		your word
sch	______		______
tz	______	______	______
	______	______	

3 Write the plural.

noodle ______
strudel ______
glitch ______
waltz ______
muesli ______

4 Write the past tense.

abseil ______
blitz ______
waltz ______
plunder ______

5 Complete the table.

word	add **s**	add **ed**	add **ing**
abseil			
blitz			
waltz			
plunder			

6 These sentences do not make sense. Change one word to a list word to make the sentences right. Then write an example of your own.

The clothes aren't washed because the machine is kaboom. ________________

My little brother will start kindness next year. ________________

Mum has gone to the definition to buy some meats and cheese for the party. ________________

Adu bleached the test: he had the highest score in the grade. ________________

I love reading travel stories because they satisfy my wardrobe. ________________

As part of the outdoor activity camp, we will learn to absolute down a wall. ________________

Dad says that when he was growing up, his birthday treat was chicken schnitzel with apple schedule. ________________

____

____

7 What do these abbreviations stand for?

UTC ____

BCE ____

AEST ____

ETA ____

e.g. ____

etc ____

i.e. ____

8 Flash fiction is a very short story. Write a flash fiction narrative about an adventure. How many list words can you use?

____

____

____

____

____

____

____

____

____

____

Answer: c

Unit 33

What activity is a modern-day version of sword fighting?

a chess
b fencing
c knitting

Say Listen Look Understand Remember Practise	
gnome	______
gnaw	______
pneumonia	______
pterodactyl	______
psychology	______
subtle	______
succumb	______
solemn	______
receipt	______
resign	______
island	______
handsome	______
exhibit	______
knack	______
playwright	______

1 Write the missing silent letter.

__rap	lis__en	__nock
bus__ness	s__ord	__riggle
i__land	plum__er	__naw
si__n	recei__t	ex__austed
__nit	__rong	bom__
autum__	__rinkle	ex__ibit

Tip

Isle and **aisle** are homophones.
isle = a small body of land surrounded by water; shortened form of island
aisle = passageway in a theatre or supermarket

2 Colour the correct homophone.

Uncle Soo likes an [isle | aisle] seat so he can stretch his legs.

Grandpa rows his boat to the [isle | aisle] in the river every summer.

3 Use the clues to find words with the same silent letter. Write the letter in the circle.

◯ _ _ _ _ _ a garden dwarf; _ _ _ _ _ _ quit a job; _ _ _ _ _ _ grind teeth together; _ _ _ _ chew on something hard

◯ _ _ _ _ _ _ a vertical row; _ _ _ _ _ _ serious; _ _ _ _ song sung in church; _ _ _ _ _ _ season after summer

◯ _ _ _ _ money you owe; _ _ _ _ _ _ _ _ not sure; _ _ _ _ _ _ _ give in; _ _ _ _ _ _ indirect, not obvious

◯ _ _ _ _ _ a weapon; _ _ _ _ _ _ _ a crease; _ _ _ _ _ ruin of a ship; _ _ _ _ _ _ circular arrangement of flowers

◯ _ _ _ _ _ _ _ statement of payment; _ _ _ _ _ _ _ _ _ lung infection; _ _ _ _ _ _ _ _ _ _ study of mind and behaviour

Spelling Rules! Student Book 5 (ISBN 9780655092711) © Janelle Ho, Helen Pearson

4 Use the clues to write the names of five body parts that have a silent letter.

finger joint _ _ _ _ _ _ _

part of the hand _ _ _ _ _

between hand and arm _ _ _ _ _

between upper and lower leg _ _ _ _

part of the lower leg _ _ _ _

5 These pairs of words belong to the same word family. Draw a circle around each silent letter. If the letter is silent in one word of a pair but pronounced in the other, draw a square around the letter that is pronounced.

autumn – autumnal	wrap – unwrap
honesty – dishonesty	resign – resignation
solemn – solemnity	soft – soften
castle – castellated	receipt – receptive

6 Make compound words. Write the meaning of each word.

play + wright ______________________________

ship + wright ______________________________

What does **wright** mean? ______________________________

7 Use silent letters to complete the riddles.

Q: Why should you never carry two fifty-cent coins in your pocket?

A: Two halves make a __hole and you might lose your money.

Q: What is a __night's favourite fish?

A: S__ordfish.

Q: What did the skeleton say when it got a com__ for Christmas?

A: I'll never part with it!

Q: What do you get when a young sheep gives a karate demonstration?

A: A lam__ chop.

Q: What did the elf say when he returned from holidays?

A: It's good to be __nome!

Hi ya!

Answer: b

Unit 34

A **poly**glot is:
a someone who eats parrots.
b a figure with many angles and sides.
c a person who speaks many languages.

Say Listen Look Understand Remember Practise	
monopoly	______
monolith	______
monologue	______
monosyllabic	______
multiple	______
multipurpose	______
multimedia	______
multicultural	______
multilingual	______
polygon	______
polyphonic	______
omnivore	______
omnipresent	______
omnipotent	______
omniscient	______

Tip A **word element** is a part of a word that can only be used in combination with another part of a word.

1 Draw a line to match the word element with its meaning.

mono	all
multi	one
omni	many

Which of the word elements above means the same as **poly**?

______

2 Underline the syllable that is stressed.

monolith
monotonous

multiple
multicultural

omnivore
omnivorous

polygon
polyphonic

Tip **Multi** is Latin in origin and **poly** is Greek. Early Greek expertise in mathematics and science means that many words in these areas start with **poly**, not **multi**.
polygon *polyester*

3 Write words beginning with these word elements.

mono / bi / multi → lingual

mono / tri / poly → syllabic

tri / quadru / multi → ple

______ ______ ______
______ ______ ______
______ ______ ______

Spelling Rules! Student Book 5 (ISBN 9780655092711) © Janelle Ho, Helen Pearson

4 Use a dictionary to find the meaning of each word. Write the meaning, then name some animals in each category. Add the suffix **ous** and use the word as an adjective in a sentence.

herbivore: ______________________________

____

____

carnivore: ______________________________

____

____

omnivore: ______________________________

____

____

Tip Mrs Malaprop was a character in a play who continually mixed up similar-sounding words. These 'slips of the tongue' are now called *malapropisms.*

5 Circle the malapropism in each sentence, then write the correct word.

I don't like Rap 'n' Roar's latest song. It's got a strong rhythm but it gets monolingual.

____

Triangles and squares are examples of polyglots. ______________

Big Brother is omnivorous: he knows everything. ______________

We use the multiparty hall for basketball, badminton and assemblies. ______________

There are multiplied ways of doing this. You just need to choose one. ______________

My brother's favourite board game is Monotony. ______________

Now write a deliberate malapropism of your own.

____

6 Monopoly is one of the most popular board games in the world. Explain how it got its name. Use a dictionary if you need help.

____

____

____

Answer: c

Unit 35 Revision

What equipment is used in the sport of curling, famous in Scotland?

a round stones and ice
b a snuggly bed and a doona
c curling tongs

1 Make a new word by adding a suffix from the box. Use each suffix at least once.

–some –ship –ion –ness –ive –y –ful –ous –ial

appreciate	________	fury	________	confident	________
wrinkle	________	artifice	________	flavour	________
carnivore	________	companion	________	exhibit	________
calm	________	resign	________	citizen	________
expense	________	trouble	________	doubt	________

2 These sentences have a redundant word or phrase. Rewrite each sentence without the redundancy.

The fake flavours were artificial.

____

The school hired the multilingual teacher who could speak many languages.

____

The debate was confusing because the illogical arguments made no sense.

____

3 Each word is missing the same sound. Add **c**, **ch**, **ck** or **k**.

flo___	strea___
ba___wards	___rome
___ree___	s___ool
___riti___al	___emist
wee___ly	lo___al

4 Make a word by adding **mis**, **dis** or **anti**.

____appear	____clockwise
____organised	____use
____biotic	____adventure
____satisfied	____leading
____appointment	____miss

5 Change each verb to an adjective by adding **able** or **ible**.

flex	________	desire	________	rely	________
admire	________	notice	________	value	________
collapse	________	reverse	________	manage	________

6 Which one of the underlined consonants needs to be doubled? Write each word correctly.

sucesful ____________	paralel ____________	exagerate ____________
acidental ____________	inapropriate ____________	ocupation ____________
necesary ____________	oposite ____________	iminent ____________

7 These words were originally French. Match each word to its picture.

surveillance silhouette biscuit

____________ ____________ ____________

8 Each sentence contains the hidden name of a city or country. Circle the letters that spell the name or that sound like the name. Write the name of the city or country correctly at the end.

Oh no! First I broke my zipper, then the buttons popped off. *Perth*

Don't forget your coat or you'll be chilly. *Chile*

The jeweller traded only in diamonds and rubies. ____________

Wash your hands often because you may pick up a germ any time. ____________

When I saw the snake I ran away. ____________

Fran celebrated her birthday at the beach. ____________

I wish this pain in my hand would go away. ____________

The timber lining in our hallway was rotten. ____________

When glandular fever struck Ching, she was ill for several days. ____________

9 Proofread this text. The text has six words that are incorrect. Circle the mistakes. Then write the correct spelling of the words in the boxes.

In summer mosquitos are such a nuisance. The whinning sound is annoying and whenever one gets me, the bite itchs like crazy. My little brother usualy gets bitten even worst than me. Mum warns him that if he keeps scratching, he will have permenent scars. He is thinking of inventing a machine to keep them away!

Answer: a

List words in unit order

Unit 1
viruses
geniuses
biases
stitches
mattresses
quizzes
sandwiches
scarves
valleys
chimneys
factories
priorities
handkerchiefs
volcanoes
fiascos

Unit 2
cacti
fungi
stimuli
syllabi
analyses
theses
parentheses
crises
lice
oxen
antennae
larvae
bacteria
series
species

Unit 3
scornful
skilful
wilful
resentful
deceitful
delightful
suspenseful
successful
plentiful
priceless
faultless
flawless
regardless
ruthless
reckless

Unit 4
instrument
experiment
implement
achievement
equipment
advertisement
boredom
wisdom
hardship
sportsmanship
censorship
insertion
hesitation
collision
aggression

Unit 5
curious
conscous
anonymous
victorious
luxurious
contagious
marvellous
venomous
ridiculous
mischievous
hideous
courteous
courageous
outrageous
miscellaneous

Unit 7
echo
scheme
chemist
monarch
scholar
chaos
chronic
chlorine
headache
architect
mechanic
technology
orchestra
archaeology
arachnophobia

Unit 8
mineral
medical
occasional
official
hysterical
historical
artificial
identical
exceptional
eventual
tragic
automatic
sympathetic
aquatic
rhythmic

Unit 9
mineral
medical
occasional
official
hysterical
historical
artificial
identical
exceptional
eventual
tragic
automatic
sympathetic
aquatic
rhythmic

Unit 10
opposite
different
applause
intelligent
excess
apparent
accidental
immediate
occupation
exaggerate
community
parallel
cannibal
innovative
affectionate

Unit 11
scuba
radar
sonar
laser
smog
heliport
lamington
diesel
bikini
braille
pasteurised
silhouette
guillotine
saxophone
valentine

Unit 13
gawky
awkward
ordinary
organise
orphan
original
orchard
ornament
orthodontist
naughty
aural
audible
audition
exhaustion
authentic

Unit 14
combine
companion
commemorate
comprehend
compel
conceal
concentrate
condescending
conference
consequence
antiseptic
antibiotic
anticlimax
antisocial
anticlockwise

Unit 15
imperfect
impatient
impractical
immature
insane
inappropriate
inconvenient
incapable
indigestible
irregular
irrelevant
irresponsible
irresistible
illegal
illogical

Unit 16
excellence
undeserved
reassuring
irresponsibly
unembarrassed
knowledgeably
acknowledgement
imaginative
dependable
discontentment
misfortunes
inconveniently
disastrously
fascination
misbehaviour

Unit 17
kiwi
batik
trek
yoga
bazaar
mandarin
spaghetti
kayak
moccasin
tsunami
sushi
kimono
bonsai
karate
origami

Spelling Rules! Student Book 5 (ISBN 9780655092711) © Janelle Ho, Helen Pearson

bouquet
camouflage
corroboree
kaleidoscope
llama
poncho

Unit 19

aqua
liquid
frequent
quality
quantity
quiver
conquest
acquire
adequate
tranquil
eloquent
quotation
quarantine
inquisitive
acquaintance

Unit 20

tongue
rogue
plague
colleague
fatigue
intrigue
dialogue
catalogue
synagogue
unique
antique
technique
boutique
mosque
plaque

Unit 21

fluid
ruin
suitcase
guide
guilty
biscuit
pursuit
suitable

guitar
inquire
bruise
intuition
nuisance mosquito
circuit

Unit 22

flour
course
flavour
favourite
colourful
humour
harbour
journal
nourish
honour
odour
mournful
detour
behaviour
tournament

Unit 23

popular
manual
library
inhabit
universe
delicate
circular
equator
benefit
democracy
dependent
monotonous
microscope
magnificent
contradict

Unit 25

admit
permit
submit
emit
impress
compress
repress
suppress

offer
refer
prefer
infer
confer
suffer
transfer

Unit 26

type
byte
rhyme
myth
gypsy
rhythm
oxygen
symbol
synthetic
typical
pyjamas
physician
sympathy
century
tragedy

Unit 27

variety
poverty
charity
creativity
simplicity
sincerity
personality
maturity
majority
minority
electricity
familiarity
speciality
opportunity
authority

Unit 28

brilliant
ignorant
dominant
tolerant
hesitant
dependant
redundant

obedient
consistent
incident
permanent
sufficient
efficient
coherent
imminent

Unit 29

distance
balance
assistance
resistance
significance
reluctance
insurance
surveillance
maintenance
influence
experience
violence
existence
evidence
conscience

Unit 31

machinery
schedule
tissue
tension
ferocious
suspicious
appreciate
luscious
commercial
initiate
confidential
influential
complexion
ambitious
conscientious

Unit 32

noodle
hamburger
schnitzel
strudel
muesli
pretzel

delicatessen
kindergarten
abseil
blitz
rucksack
wanderlust
uber
kaput
waltz

Unit 33

gnome
gnaw
pneumonia
pterodactyl
psychology
subtle
succumb
solemn
receipt
resign
island
handsome
exhibit
knack
playwright

Unit 34

monopoly
monolith
monologue
monosyllabic
multiple
multipurpose
multimedia
multicultural
multilingual
polygon
polyphonic
omnivore
omnipresent
omnipotent
omniscient

LIST WORDS IN ALPHABETICAL ORDER

abseil	Unit 32
accidental	Unit 10
achievement	Unit 4
acknowledgement	Unit 16
acquaintance	Unit 19
acquire	Unit 19
adequate	Unit 19
adorable	Unit 9
admit	Unit 25
advertisement	Unit 4
affectionate	Unit 10
aggression	Unit 4
ambitious	Unit 31
analyses	Unit 2
anonymous	Unit 5
antennae	Unit 2
antibiotic	Unit 14
anticlimax	Unit 14
anticlockwise	Unit 14
antique	Unit 20
antiseptic	Unit 14
antisocial	Unit 14
apparent	Unit 10
applause	Unit 10
appreciate	Unit 31
aqua	Unit 19
aquatic	Unit 8
arachnophobia	Unit 7
archaeology	Unit 7
architect	Unit 7
artificial	Unit 8
assistance	Unit 29
audible	Unit 13
audition	Unit 13
aural	Unit 13
authentic	Unit 13
authority	Unit 27
automatic	Unit 8
available	Unit 9
awkward	Unit 13
bacteria	Unit 2
balance	Unit 29
batik	Unit 17
bazaar	Unit 17
behaviour	Unit 21
benefit	Unit 23
biases	Unit 1
bikini	Unit 11
biscuit	Unit 21
blitz	Unit 32
bonsai	Unit 17
boredom	Unit 4
bouquet	Unit 17
boutique	Unit 20
braille	Unit 11
brilliant	Unit 28
bruise	Unit 21
byte	Unit 26
cacti	Unit 2
camouflage	Unit 17
cannibal	Unit 10
capable	Unit 9
catalogue	Unit 20
censorship	Unit 4
century	Unit 26
chaos	Unit 7
charity	Unit 27
chemist	Unit 7
chimneys	Unit 1
chlorine	Unit 7
chronic	Unit 7
circuit	Unit 21
circular	Unit 23
coherent	Unit 28
colleague	Unit 20
collision	Unit 4
colourful	Unit 21
combine	Unit 14
comfortable	Unit 9
commemorate	Unit 14
commercial	Unit 31
community	Unit 10
companion	Unit 14
compel	Unit 14
complexion	Unit 31
comprehend	Unit 14
compress	Unit 25
conceal	Unit 14
concentrate	Unit 14
condescending	Unit 14
confer	Unit 25
conference	Unit 14
confidential	Unit 31
conquest	Unit 19
conscience	Unit 29
conscientious	Unit 31
conscious	Unit 5
consequence	Unit 14
consistent	Unit 28
contagious	Unit 5
contradict	Unit 23
corroboree	Unit 17
courageous	Unit 5
course	Unit 21
courteous	Unit 5
creativity	Unit 27
crises	Unit 2
curious	Unit 5
deceitful	Unit 3
delicate	Unit 23
delicatessen	Unit 32
delightful	Unit 3
democracy	Unit 23
dependable	Unit 16
dependant	Unit 28
dependent	Unit 23
detour	Unit 21
dialogue	Unit 20
diesel	Unit 11
different	Unit 10
disastrously	Unit 16
discontentment	Unit 16
distance	Unit 29
dominant	Unit 28
echo	Unit 7
efficient	Unit 28
electricity	Unit 27
eligible	Unit 9
eloquent	Unit 19
emit	Unit 25
equator	Unit 23
equipment	Unit 4
eventual	Unit 8
evidence	Unit 29
exaggerate	Unit 10
excellence	Unit 16
exceptional	Unit 8
excess	Unit 10
exhaustion	Unit 13
exhibit	Unit 33
existence	Unit 29
experience	Unit 29
experiment	Unit 4
factories	Unit 1
familiarity	Unit 27
fascination	Unit 16
fatigue	Unit 20
faultless	Unit 3
favourite	Unit 21
ferocious	Unit 31
fiascos	Unit 1
flavour	Unit 21
flawless	Unit 3
flexible	Unit 9
flour	Unit 21
fluid	Unit 21
frequent	Unit 19
fungi	Unit 2
gawky	Unit 13
geniuses	Unit 1
gnaw	Unit 33
gnome	Unit 33
guide	Unit 21
guillotine	Unit 11
guilty	Unit 21
guitar	Unit 21
gypsy	Unit 26
hamburger	Unit 32
handkerchiefs	Unit 1
handsome	Unit 33
harbour	Unit 21
hardship	Unit 4
headache	Unit 7
heliport	Unit 11
hesitant	Unit 28
hesitation	Unit 4
hideous	Unit 5
historical	Unit 8
honour	Unit 21
horrible	Unit 9
humour	Unit 21
hysterical	Unit 8
identical	Unit 8
ignorant	Unit 28
illegal	Unit 15
illegible	Unit 9
illogical	Unit 15
imaginative	Unit 16
immature	Unit 15
immediate	Unit 10
imminent	Unit 28
impatient	Unit 15
imperfect	Unit 15
implement	Unit 4
impossible	Unit 9
impractical	Unit 15
impress	Unit 25
inappropriate	Unit 15
incapable	Unit 15
incident	Unit 28
inconvenient	Unit 15
inconveniently	Unit 16
indigestible	Unit 15
infer	Unit 25
influence	Unit 29
influential	Unit 31
inhabit	Unit 23
initiate	Unit 31
innovative	Unit 10
inquire	Unit 21
inquisitive	Unit 19
insane	Unit 15
insertion	Unit 4
instrument	Unit 4
insurance	Unit 29
intelligent	Unit 10
intrigue	Unit 20
intuition	Unit 21
invisible	Unit 9
irregular	Unit 15
irrelevant	Unit 15
irresistible	Unit 15
irresponsible	Unit 15
irresponsibly	Unit 16
island	Unit 33
journal	Unit 21

Ha ha ha

kaput Unit 32
karate Unit 17
kayak Unit 17
kimono Unit 17
kindergarten Unit 32
kiwi Unit 17
knack Unit 33
knowledgeably Unit 16

lamington Unit 11
larvae Unit 2
laser Unit 11
library Unit 23
lice Unit 2
liquid Unit 19
llama Unit 17
luscious Unit 31
luxurious Unit 5

machinery Unit 31
magnificent Unit 23
maintenance Unit 29
majority Unit 27
mandarin Unit 17
manual Unit 23
marvellous Unit 5
mattresses Unit 1
maturity Unit 27
mechanic Unit 7
medical Unit 8
microscope Unit 23
mineral Unit 8
minority Unit 27
misbehaviour Unit 16
miscellaneous Unit 5
mischievous Unit 5
miserable Unit 9
misfortunes Unit 16
moccasin Unit 17
monarch Unit 7
monolith Unit 34
monologue Unit 34
monopoly Unit 34
monosyllabic Unit 34
monotonous Unit 23
mosque Unit 20
mosquito Unit 21
mournful Unit 21
muesli Unit 32
multicultural Unit 34
multilingual Unit 34
multimedia Unit 34
multiple Unit 34
multipurpose Unit 34
myth Unit 26

naughty Unit 13
noodle Unit 32
nourish Unit 21
nuisance Unit 21

obedient Unit 28
occasional Unit 8
occupation Unit 10
odour Unit 21
offer Unit 25
official Unit 8
omnipotent Unit 34
omnipresent Unit 34
omniscient Unit 34
omnivore Unit 34
opportunity Unit 27
opposite Unit 10
orchard Unit 13
orchestra Unit 7
ordinary Unit 13
organise Unit 13
origami Unit 17
original Unit 13
ornament Unit 13
orphan Unit 13
orthodontist Unit 13
outrageous Unit 5
oxen Unit 2
oxygen Unit 26

parallel Unit 10
parentheses Unit 2
pasteurised Unit 11
permanent Unit 28
permit Unit 25
personality Unit 27
physician Unit 26
plague Unit 20
plaque Unit 20
playwright Unit 33
plentiful Unit 3
pneumonia Unit 33
polygon Unit 34
polyphonic Unit 34
poncho Unit 17
popular Unit 23
poverty Unit 27
prefer Unit 25
pretzel Unit 32
priceless Unit 3
priorities Unit 1
psychology Unit 33
pterodactyl Unit 33
pursuit Unit 21
pyjamas Unit 26

quality Unit 19
quantity Unit 19
quarantine Unit 19
quiver Unit 19
quizzes Unit 1
quotation Unit 19

radar Unit 11
reassuring Unit 16
receipt Unit 33
reckless Unit 3
redundant Unit 28
refer Unit 25
regardless Unit 3
reliable Unit 9
reluctance Unit 29
repress Unit 25
resentful Unit 3
resign Unit 33
resistance Unit 29
rhyme Unit 26
rhythm Unit 26
rhythmic Unit 8
ridiculous Unit 5
rogue Unit 20
rucksack Unit 32
ruin Unit 21
ruthless Unit 3

sandwiches Unit 1
saxophone Unit 11
scarves Unit 1
schedule Unit 31
scheme Unit 7
schnitzel Unit 32
scholar Unit 7
scornful Unit 3
scuba Unit 11
sensible Unit 9
series Unit 2
significance Unit 29
silhouette Unit 11
simplicity Unit 27
sincerity Unit 27
skilful Unit 3
smog Unit 11
solemn Unit 33
sonar Unit 11
spaghetti Unit 17
speciality Unit 27
species Unit 2
sportsmanship Unit 4
stimuli Unit 2
stitches Unit 1
strudel Unit 32
submit Unit 25
subtle Unit 33
successful Unit 3
succumb Unit 33
suffer Unit 25
sufficient Unit 28
suitable Unit 21
suitcase Unit 21
suppress Unit 25
surveillance Unit 29
sushi Unit 17
suspenseful Unit 3
suspicious Unit 31
syllabi Unit 2
symbol Unit 26
sympathetic Unit 8
sympathy Unit 26
synagogue Unit 20
synthetic Unit 26

technique Unit 20
technology Unit 7
tension Unit 31
terrible Unit 9
theses Unit 2
tissue Unit 31
tolerant Unit 28
tongue Unit 20
tournament Unit 21
tragedy Unit 26
tragic Unit 8
tranquil Unit 19
transfer Unit 25
trek Unit 17
tsunami Unit 17
type Unit 26
typical Unit 26

uber Unit 32
undeserved Unit 16
unembarrassed Unit 16
unique Unit 20
universe Unit 23

valentine Unit 11
valleys Unit 1
valuable Unit 9
variety Unit 27
venomous Unit 5
victorious Unit 5
violence Unit 29
viruses Unit 1
volcanoes Unit 1

waltz Unit 32
wanderlust Unit 32
wilful Unit 3
wisdom Unit 4

yoga Unit 17

SPELLING RULES AND TIPS

- Some words of foreign origin change the vowel or vowels to show the plural.
  Some nouns of Greek origin that end in **us** change **us** to **i**. *cactus → cacti*
  Exceptions: *octopus → octopi or octopuses*
  hippopotamus → hippopotami or hippopotamuses
  Some nouns of Greek origin that end in **is** change **is** to **es**. *crisis → crises*
  Some nouns of Latin origin that end in **a** add **e**. *larva → larvae*
  Some nouns of Latin origin that end in **um** change **um** to **a**. *curriculum → curricula*

- The suffixes **ment**, **dom**, **ship** and **hood** all form nouns. The base word does not usually change when these suffixes are added.

- Most words that end in **ic** add **al** and **ly** to form the adverb. *magic → magically*
  Exception: *public → publicly*

- Words that end in **ous** are adjectives.
  If the base word ends in **e**, drop the **e** before adding **ous**. *fame → famous*
  Exception: words ending in **ce** or **ge**.
  If the base words ends in **our**, drop the **u** before adding **ous**. *humour → humorous*
  If the base word ends in **ce** or **y**, change the **e** or **y** to **i** before adding **ous**.
  space → spacious *vary → various*

- If the base word ends in silent e, the e is usually dropped before adding **ible** or **able**.
  believable *collapsible*
  Keep the **e** to keep the soft **c** or soft **g** sound. *noticeable* *changeable*

- The prefixes **in** and **un** can be used in front of base words beginning with most letters.
  im is only used in front of **m** or **p**. *immortal* *impossible*
  ir is only used in front of **r**. *irreversible*
  il is only used in front of **l**. *illegible*

- If the adjective ends in **ent**, the noun usually ends in **ence**. *violent → violence*
  If the adjective ends in **ant**, the noun usually ends in **ance**. *distant → distance*
  Some nouns end in **ency** or **ancy**. *urgency* *hesitancy*

- Antonyms can be made by:
  - adding a prefix *helpful → unhelpful*
  - changing the suffix. *careful → careless*

Spelling Rules! Student Book 5 (ISBN 9780655092711) © Janelle Ho, Helen Pearson